She Has
Washed
My Feet
with
Her Tears

She Has Washed My Feet with Her Tears

New Testament Stories of Women's Faith and Rebellion

Ross Saunders

Seastone

BERKELEY, CALIFORNIA

To my wife Stavroula
for her unfailing support and encouragement,
and to all those rebellious women in Christian congregations
who continue to assert their right to respond as women.

Published by: Seastone, an imprint of Ulysses Press
P.O. Box 3440
Berkeley, CA 94703-3440

First published in 1996 by E. J. Dwyer

Library of Congress Cataloging-in-Publication Data
Sauders, Ross.
    She has washed my feet with her tears : New Testament stories of women's faith and rebellion / Ross Saunders.
        p.   cm.
    Includes bibliographical references and index.
    ISBN 1-56975-161-7 (alk. paper)
        1. Women in the Bible.   2. Bible.   N.T.--Criticism, interpretation, etc.
    3. Woman (Christian theology)--Biblical teaching.   I. Title.
BS2445.S28   1998   98-36089
225.9'22'082--dc21   CIP

Printed in the U.S.A. by Banta Book Group

10 9 8 7 6 5 4 3 2 1

Editorial and production staff: Tom Hinds, Steven Schwartz, Lily Chou
Design: Sarah Levin, Leslie Henriques
Cover art: William Hole, *The Life of Jesus of Nazareth*

Distributed in the United States by Publishers Group West, in Canada by Raincoast Books, and in Great Britain and Europe by World Leisure Marketing

Table of Contents

Introduction

If you were asked to name a rebellious woman in the New Testament you would no doubt mention either Herodias or her daughter Salome.

Herodias wiggled her hips and flashed her black eyes at her powerful brother-in-law King Herod so often that he broke the Jewish law, marrying her while her divorced husband Philip was still alive. She maintained her grip on Herod when John the Baptist exposed their misalliance, encouraging her daughter Salome to demand the Baptist's head on a silver platter after Salome provocatively danced Herod into erotic powerlessness.

But I have in mind a much different kind of rebelliousness. I mean being rebellious to the extent of breaking with man-made convention and demanding to be heard, seen, or allowed to carry out actions normally permitted only to men, executing those actions at times when men were inhibited from taking up responsibilities they had arrogated to themselves in the first place.

The same phenomenon can be seen in many indigenous groups around the world today: rebellious women are leading their people in the struggle for equality and human rights. Rebellious, because they dare to step outside the position society has constructed for them.

Because we are not very familiar with the place of women in the Mediterranean society of the New Testament period, we may fail to see the large number of rebellious women who feature in the life of the early church.

In Chapter One of the book I describe the place of women in Mediterranean societies of the first century of our era. In Chapter Two I focus on those women who are named in the gospels, while in Chapter Three I discuss those named in the book of Acts. In Chapter Four I concentrate on those named in the epistles. In Chapters Five and Six I examine how Paul constructed the place of women in the early congregations, and in Chapter Seven I show how women disappear almost entirely from the early post-apostolic church.

one

Mediterranean Societies

It's easy to read about the people who lived in the first century of our era and think we can readily understand them by simply putting our own minds into their heads. We figure people haven't changed all that much over the centuries. We just need to make allowances for language, technology and communications, and there they are: reflections of ourselves!

Sociologists have tried to make our task easier. Their studies of nineteenth- and twentieth-century communities have led them to devise models that explain how people behave in given situations and societies. But when they tried to apply these models to older societies, they found they didn't quite work. In the process of adapting and refining the models to account for older societies, they fell into the trap of reading their own mindset back into the ancient world, with the inevitable result that the ancients started to look and talk like us.

The same problem showed up when scholars began translating the classical writings: Plato began sounding like Descartes and Euripides like Shakespeare!

Anthropologists have long tried to study ancient societies and understand them on their own terms. They have made honest efforts to analyze the way traditional societies have operated. Cultural anthropologists, in particular, have tried to include a broader perspective, searching for ways to enter the mindset of people of different centuries and with histories different from our own.

Putting some of these disciplines together, it is now more possible than ever to eavesdrop, so to speak, on people of earlier times whose histories took different paths than ours. We are the strangers—not they. We are the foreigners traveling back in time, standing on the outskirts of their villages and towns, walking up and down their marketplaces, listening in to their conversations and watching with awe their social rituals and ceremonies, struggling to understand them on their own terms, in their own words.

What I want to do is outline those social aspects of the Mediterranean world that will help you understand the place of women, and show how early Christianity went about trying to change some of the social relationships that seemed inappropriate for Christians.

The Mediterranean Model

What the cultural anthropologists have discovered is that all the societies that lived around the Mediterranean Sea during the period of the Greek and Roman empires shared many cultural concepts. In spite of local language differences, the Greek language remained the lingua franca for many centuries, especially during the first century of our era. Thus we can refer to these people as "typical Mediterraneans," whether they came from Greece, Italy, North Africa, Spain, Egypt, Israel, western Asia or the various islands in the Mediterranean, Ionian and Aegean seas.

Here, then, are four core values of these societies. And for each core value there were strategies—what the anthropologists call "means values"—for maintaining those core values.

Honor and Shame

"Honor" is a combination of your assessment of your place in the community plus the community's assessment of your place.

In the first-century Mediterranean world everyone belonged in a great procession: the most honored person at one end, the least honored at the other. Your place in the procession was determined almost exclusively by the status of your father, your family and tribe. Each person was expected to act in ways appropriate to their status. Attempts to act in ways that seemed aimed at moving your place in the procession toward the head would cause you to be jeered at—even dishonored. No one, of course, wanted to go further down the line!

But there were acceptable ways in which you could advance yourself. You could become an athlete, compete in games and win. This would result in your being attributed *arete*—excellence. While you kept on winning, your *arete* would guarantee you a place somewhat ahead of your natural rank in the procession. But once you came second, you lost all your *arete* and would be returned to your normal position.

If you were a man, you could try and become a religious teacher—a scribe. But if you came from a place far down the procession, you would need the patronage of someone near the head of the procession, making you permanently in that patron's debt.

If you were a peasant and therefore near the bottom end of the procession, you could train to become an artisan—a carpenter, stonemason, leather worker, potter, etc. But trades such as these advanced you only one or two places up, since generally artisans were not accorded much honor at all. While artisans were in constant demand and their products valued, they themselves had lowly status. The problem you would face is that, if you happened to be the eldest son in the family, you were expected to follow in your father's trade or position. If your father happened to be a peasant share farmer and you decided to become a carpenter, the moment you left home to learn carpentry your father and your family name would be dishonored. Also, you had no place of honor until your father died, when you would take over as family head and as maintainer of the family's place of honor in the procession.

It is worth remembering here that Jesus himself dishonored his dead father Joseph's name when he left home to begin his mission. He was thus a cause of offense to his home town, Nazareth. This explains the reaction of his fellow villagers when, after his baptism and testing in the wilderness, he returned to Nazareth and went to the synagogue where he had gone since he was a child. At first they listened in awe to his words, but then they remembered how he had left home, dishonored his father's name, and left his mother and unmarried sisters to fend for themselves instead of being their sponsor and caretaker.[1]

And when Jesus called his first disciples, there were several who were eldest sons. He called upon them to act in a way that was considered dishonorable when he insisted they leave home and follow him.

It was not sufficient just to be aware of your place in the status procession. You were expected to maintain your honor by acknowledging your community and making sure you kept that community in its place relative to neighboring communities.

If you happened to own your own land and house, you were expected to make donations to your community institutions. In the case of the Jewish communities we are most interested in, this could involve endowing lectureships for scribes to come from Jerusalem and teach in your local synagogue; providing money for new furniture for your synagogue; paying for the replacement of a worn-out scroll; paying for a memorial to a famous religious leader, and so on.

In doing any of these things your name would be written up for all to see that you had fulfilled your duty of honor maintenance. The higher up your place in the procession, the more you would be expected to share with your community.

It is important here to understand that gifts of money to help the poor were not regarded as honor maintenance. While the community leaders were in a position to reciprocate by paying for your name to be inscribed in stone or wood, the poor would not be able to do so.

When the rich young ruler came to Jesus and asked what he should do to inherit eternal life, he was told to sell everything and give to the poor. Had this young man of high status done what Jesus commanded, he would have dishonored himself in two ways in the eyes of his community. In the first place, selling everything his father had left him would have made giving gifts to his community impossible. In the second, giving everything away to the poor would have brought him more dishonor, as no one regarded giving to the poor an honorable action. The poor were born that way and deserved only to stay in their poverty. The only ones that you helped were those of your own status who had lost their money because of a war or a bad investment. You did that because one day you might need them to reciprocate.

This young man could not face a life of being dishonored, and so he walked away sadly. It needs to be remembered that he was attached to his honor and not to his money and possessions: the money was what allowed him to maintain his honorable status in the eyes of himself and his community.

Another means of maintaining your honor was to practice hospitality. You would regularly entertain with dinners. You would invite to your dinner only those on the same social level as you. You would select your guest list carefully and make it public, so that those you had not invited would know. You would expect those you invited to invite you in turn.

Dinners and feasts were a very important means of signaling your own social status and demonstrating that you accepted the responsibility of maintaining your honorable status in your community. You would never invite anyone below you to dinner, for that would risk being dishonored. Nor would you invite anyone above you, for that could mean you were pretending to be on a higher level than you actually were.

We should understand, then, that hospitality did not arise from any desire to help those in need nor to express friendship. When the New Testament exhorts Christians to be hospitable, we must understand it to mean the sort of hospitality not based on honor maintenance, but on the responsibility of sharing one's blessings with others and meeting their needs, irrespective of their social standing in relation to yours.

Maintaining one's honorable position in the eyes of the community was the single most powerful driving force in the whole of the first-century Mediterranean world.

Only males were accorded honor. Women were recognized only in relationship to some man—a father, an uncle, a grandfather, a brother, a husband, a son. They had no honor: they reflected the honor of the man who was their sponsor. But they had a sense of shame. Their primary role was to protect their sponsor's honor by behaving in a positive, virginal manner. They must be careful that in public they dressed and behaved demurely, spoke to men only when spoken to, were seen only with men who were of the same status as their sponsor, and stayed in circumstances that could not be misconstrued.

The physical virginity of a woman was important as it symbolized her sense of shame. Only her groom could break that barrier and thus claim her as his honorable partner. Women could not take part in sport of any kind, not only because Greek and Roman games expected nudity of the competitors, but also because excessive physical activity could rupture the hymen and place the woman's virginity in serious doubt.

Any woman who did not act in appropriate ways would bring shame to her male sponsor. Since she had no honor in her own right to maintain, her role was to help maintain her male sponsor's honor.

Women without male sponsors were an embarrassment to the ancient world. A widow without an extended family had to become either a prostitute or a beggar: there were no other avenues of acquiring money open to her. This was the case with any single woman who suddenly lost all her male sponsors. This explains why the early church selected widows as their first social responsibility.

The core values of honor and shame are probably the most important to take into account when trying to understand the way people related to each other and their community in the first-century Mediterranean world.

Embedded Identity

Today we are so used to seeing ourselves as separate individuals with individual rights that we can easily misunderstand people's perceptions of themselves in the ancient world. They had no sense of personal identity the way we do. They did not try to understand the feelings of others either.

Every person was embedded in another person, a family, a tribe, a village, a city, a country. You were known by others as "the son of," "the daughter of," a relative of some head of the family. If you were a visitor from another place, you were "Jesus of Nazareth," "Saul of Tarsus," "Barnabas of Cyprus," and so on.

In the Mediterranean world, everyone knew about being a member of a family, a community and a village. This was their personal identity. When a slave was liberated, the slave always took on the name of a family head or of a god, in order to have an identity. A personal identity separate from anyone else was impossible and unthinkable.

When people, either Jews or gentiles, became Christians, they took their identity from their new father, God. They saw themselves as members of the family of God, the congregation, with Jesus Christ as their elder brother.

When the head of a household became a follower of Jesus, the whole household, including slaves, would naturally also do so. If a junior member of a household turned to Christ, there would be division in the household, often resulting in that member being disowned. That person would then often try and join another household who had all turned to Christ, or at least identify with a congregation.

We will never understand how society worked in New Testament times until we come to terms with their lack of individualism, and with the fact that it was always someone else who established identity. This was especially the case for women. Women had no identity as women, only as related to some man. No woman ever saw herself as embedded in her mother or older sister or grandmother or any other woman. Without a male sponsor a woman had no identity or importance at all.

One of the changes Jesus brought to the society was to relate to women as though they had an identity as women. He spoke to them directly, never, as was the custom, through a father, husband, brother or son. He accepted their gifts and ministrations in spite of the appearance of shame it brought him.

We must always be on the lookout for those cases where Jesus went against the customs of his day, and for those cases where he deliberately stayed within the boundaries. When I describe particular women, I will be taking special note of these things, because they are very important in working out what was happening in the lives of these Mediterranean people. Jesus himself was a Mediterranean and was brought up in Mediterranean ways. But he saw himself embedded in his father, God, not in his deceased father Joseph.

A World of Limited Good

In this century we believe there is an infinite supply of goods and services. Even if there is a shortage of something, we simply wait a while and our need is supplied. We can buy almost anything we like by working hard to save up for it. But in the Mediterranean world, the perception was that everything was in limited supply. And that "everything" included non-tangible items like love, honor, friendship, luck and health. Because of this, you could not look to have more than your community said was your right. To try and acquire more furniture or land or sheep or friends or honorable mentions than was appropriate to your status would have been interpreted as an attempt to cut in ahead of someone else in the status procession, and you would be jeered and dishonored. Likewise, for you to have less than was your due would also have brought you disapprobation.

Your status was carefully and precisely determined, and you moved out of it at your peril.

The only way to become rich beyond your status was to take from someone else. This is one reason why the rich were criticized and despised in the New Testament. The rich became rich only at the expense of the poor. The rich created structural poverty by buying up all the arable land and then forcing peasants to work that land and surrender most of the fruits of their labor back to the landowners. Men who inherited riches were held to account because their fathers and grandfathers before them created their wealth out of the poor.

Even friends were perceived to be in limited supply. You stayed within the family and village networks. Any attempt to widen your circle of friends was perceived as trying to win people away from others and their networks.

Honor was limited. You inherited your honorable position from your father. You could not gain more honor without trying to take someone else's place in the honor stakes.

The Jews believed the love of God was limited and belonged solely to them. Gentiles had to convert to Judaism before they could share in God's love. When Jesus proclaimed that the love of God was not limited but infinite, available to all who ask for it, he was deliberately going against the perception that everything in the universe was of limited supply.

Many aspects of the way the early Christians dealt with social problems can best be understood in the light of the general perception of limited good.

Everything in Its Place

Peace and order were perceived to result from everything and everybody being accorded a proper place. In all open societies like those of the Mediterranean world, laws need to be at a minimum and customs at a maximum. Laws needed to be interpreted by specialists, while customs were imbibed with mother's milk.

So-called "purity" rules have nothing at all to do with our notion of hygiene. If something or someone is "pure," then that thing or person is in its correct place and so does not bring any harm to anyone else. But someone not in his or her proper place is perceived to be a threat to peace and order, and is therefore labeled "impure."

The Mediterranean world was preoccupied with fluids that came out of the orifices of the human body. While inside the body the fluids are in their proper place. Once they emerge from the body, they are "out of place" and therefore a potential threat to the good order of the community.

Thus blood, pus, urine, feces, saliva, mucus, perspiration, semen, tears, and breath would all be regarded as being out of place once they left the body.

Rituals were devised to recognize that these things were out of place and to help remove the perceived threat to the good order and peace of the community. Jews, like all peoples at that time, were never sure others took the same trouble to deal with these threats to order. This meant that, for example, when a Jew went to the local market to buy a new cooking pot, he would do two things when he returned home: he would ask his wife to wash the pot thoroughly, and he would take off his outer garment and put on a new one. Both these things needed to be done because he was never sure who had picked up the cooking pot or who had brushed against his cloak while he picked his way through the crowds at the market.

When a husband made love to his wife they both bathed afterward because his semen had left his body and entered hers, making her "unclean," and because some of his seminal fluid and her natural lubricant was on his body. There was also sweat and saliva from each on the other.

Even birth was a case where being "out of place" was critical. A new person, in its place inside the mother, emerged from its mother and became out of place. Elaborate rituals were engaged in to deal with the placenta and the fluids that emerged from the mother's body. The baby had to be initiated into the family. Once all these things had been attended to, the baby was in its place in the family, tribe and village, and the mother in a suitable "clean" condition to resume her place.

The Old Testament describes these rituals for Israelites in Leviticus 12. The mother is to be ritually unclean—not allowed to be with other people—for seven days if the baby is a boy. On the eighth day the baby boy is circumcised and then the mother continues to be regarded as unclean for another thirty-three days. If the baby is a girl, these periods of uncleanness are doubled. At the conclusion of her period of separation from her family, she is to bring an offering to the Lord. One can only speculate on why the mother is penalized for giving birth to a female baby.

It is important to understand these "purity" rules had nothing to do with hygiene. They were devised to ensure that the good order of the family and society was not being breached by unwanted intrusions of matter that belonged inside the human body. Since blood and amniotic fluid could continue to seep from the woman's womb for some time after childbirth, the fixed periods of ritual uncleanness were necessary to ensure that the flow had finally ended.

Another example of dealing with a person out of place is found in Deuteronomy 21:10-14. If an Israelite warrior took a fancy to a woman he had captured in battle, he could take her to his home and marry her. But first he had to shave her head, trim her nails and put new clothes on her. She had to mourn her father and mother for a month and then the warrior was free take her to his bed. As an enemy she was out of place in Israel. If she was to stay in this family, she had to undergo these indignities as part of the ritual of finding her a place in her new family. These things were all visible to the rest of the family and tribe, so that they, too, knew she was out of place and therefore not to be welcomed or related to in any way until the rituals were completed.

Order could also be breached by people of the same race but from outside the village entering the closed community. When a guest from another village arrived, there were elaborate rituals of greeting that served to recognize the guest was from another place and needed to be melded into the community so as not to be a potential threat to the order.

Jews did not enter the property of gentiles for fear of ritual contamination. Jews did not know how gentiles dealt with important things like food, clothing, human relationships and dust. Dust belonged outside on roads and footpaths. It was in place there, but when brought inside a house via the feet, sandals and clothes, it was out of place and had to be dealt with. Ritual washing of feet and sometimes putting on an outer garment were examples of dealing with out-of-place dust. A good way to insult someone was to deliberately place something considered unclean onto their garments or inside their house. To spit on someone's face or clothing was an insult, as was the shaking of your dust onto their person.

Each community made its own decisions about what were the proper places for everything and then created rituals for dealing with situations in which out-of-placeness occurred. Mammals, birds, reptiles and fish all had their proper places in Jewish life, often based upon the kind of food that entered their bodies. In each case only animals that fed solely on plant life were classified as acceptable to be eaten. Because pigs grubbed in the ground and ate rats, mice and insects, they were looked upon as potentially dangerous to good order, adding unknowns to the urine and feces of humans.

The notions of "sacred" and "profane" are also based on the concept of being out of place. Any thing or person that belonged to a divinity was in its proper place when used for that divinity; but when used for some other reason was considered out of place.

Thus, a utensil used for ritual washing during a religious ceremony was regarded as dedicated for that purpose. If used in some non-religious context, the divinity was regarded as having been dishonored or blasphemed. Utensils and people that were to be dedicated to a divinity needed a ritual performed over them to signify that their proper place was now in that sacred service. Elaborate public rituals were devised so everyone would know the proper place of the utensil or person. If some other utensil or person was used, not having been set apart for this sacred purpose, they were regarded as being out of place and not fit for the service of the divinity.

The tags "sacred" and "profane" refer, therefore, to the proper place in which the utensil or person is to operate. It is important to understand here that they do not refer to any inherent moral or spiritual quality of the utensil or person, but simply to the sphere in which each has a proper place.

Nearly all the rules of religious purity mentioned in the gospels refer to this notion. The labels "clean" and "unclean" were convenient ways of describing what was in place and what was out of place, and "sacred" and "profane" to the spheres of activity in which being in place was appropriate.

The Surrogate Family

The family of blood and kin was the foundation of Mediterranean society. Every person's identity was located within the family. When a younger son left his family to go to the city, he would try and find a family in which to re-embed himself. It would probably have no blood or kinship ties with the extended family he came from. But if there were even distant cousins in the city, he would find a natural home with them. This new family was known as his surrogate family; he would find his new identity there.

It is important to realize that Jesus often talks about the kingdom of God as a surrogate family, with God as the father and himself as the elder brother. All other members are on an equal footing as far as authority is concerned, and relate to each other much as in a natural family. This becomes important when trying to understand some of Jesus' apparently anti-family sayings. He was merely expressing that in a conflict between a person's responsibilities to the surrogate kingdom-of-God family and the natural family, the surrogate family must have first preference.

It will become obvious that in the surrogate family of the kingdom of God, women cease to be of secondary status or important only in relationship to a man. They will claim an identity in their own right as sisters of their elder brother, Christ.

Woman in Her Place

A great deal has been written about the place of women in the ancient world. I want to concentrate on those aspects that highlight their situations as reported in the New Testament.

Woman's primary and most important place was in the household. She managed the household budget and saw that the household slaves were properly supervised. She organized the food and welcoming rituals for her husband's dinners. She reared and educated the children until the boys came to puberty, when the father took over their education and discipline. It was her responsibility to see that nothing or no one out of place came into the house.

Whenever she left the house to shop or visit those within her natural network, she had to be accompanied by a suitable male, not so much to protect her, but to protect her husband's name from any slips she might make, however inadvertently, through improper conduct. Any males who wished to address her had to do so through her chaperone, not directly. A woman had to be careful when in the company of males that no perceived dishonor to her husband's name could result.

Her body belonged solely to her husband. He alone could touch her and enter her. For any other adult male to do so would bring shame and dishonor to her husband. In this sense she was sacred to him. Adultery was perceived as a sin against the husband, whereas a husband was free to touch and enter the body of any unmarried, adult, single female without incurring the charge of adultery. Such an act did not bring any shame or dishonor to him. However, should he take the virginity of the daughter of some man of higher social status, that man could sue him for damage to his reputation and honor.

Upon reaching puberty daughters were expected to marry in the order of their age, and suitable husbands would be found by their father, or by their elder brother should their father be dead. They had no choice in this matter. They brought with them a dowry commensurate with their father's position of honor in the community. This dowry passed to the ownership of the husband, who had to look after but not spend it. When he died it went to the care of his oldest son.

Jewish women were generally not permitted to go into business or to earn money. Should they do things like take in washing or do housework, the wages were placed in the hands of her male sponsor, be it father, older brother, husband or oldest son. Any daughters unmarried on the death of both parents had to go to the sponsorship of the nearest male relative, who would look after them. If there were none, they would have to beg for their living or go into prostitution, unless the village took pity on them.

Women also had to sit separately in the synagogue for worship. At social occasions women were always in the background and had to dress appropriately, that is, according to the social standing of their sponsor.

A female slave was rarely manumitted. She would be regarded as the possession of her male owner. Should she marry a fellow slave who at some point was manumitted, she was not. Her children also remained the property of her owner.

As we will see, Jesus chose to treat women rather differently in many ways, and caused a great deal of confusion in his community. The early church gave women a whole new status, until the end of the first century when women again virtually disappeared from church life. (For more detailed information on the place of women in the first century of our era, see those studies referred to in the bibliography.)

It is only when we understand something of the place of women in this ancient society can we even begin to see just how outrageous Jesus and God were in speaking and relating to women the way they did.

- - - *two* - - -

Women in the Gospels

The four gospels of the New Testament record the actions and sayings of a remarkable number of women, given the general attitude of the day toward women. And, with important exceptions, most of these women were respected within their various social classes. You have only to read ancient writers like Herodotus, Pliny and Pausanias to see the difference. Few women were mentioned, and most of those act in rather shameful ways.

One of the first things you notice about the women in the gospels is that they are named in their own right as persons. Since a woman's only identity came from her male sponsor—father, husband, uncle, grandfather, son, etc.—she was always named with her sponsor. But the only time women are named in this way in the gospels is when their sponsor is also an important part of the narrative. Most of the time, the woman was treated as if her name was all that was needed to affirm her identity.

This fact alone shows Christianity made an initial, radical move toward giving women a separate status from that of men.

I have divided the women in the gospels into a number of categories in order to show that not only were the leaders of the church, beginning with Jesus himself, affirming the right of women to a separate identity, but also the women themselves were beginning to feel God had given them a right to assert themselves.

Demanding to be Heard

The Syro-Phoenician Woman

And Jesus went away from there and withdrew to the district of Tyre and Sidon. And behold, a Canaanite woman from that region came out and cried, "Have mercy on me, O Lord, Son of David; my daughter is severely possessed by a demon." But he did not answer her a word. And his disciples came and begged him, saying, "Send her away, for she is crying after us." He answered, "I was sent only to the lost sheep of the house of Israel." But she came and knelt before him, saying, "Lord, help me." And he answered, "It is not fair to take the children's bread and throw it to the dogs." She said, "Yes, Lord, yet even the dogs eat the crumbs that fall from their master's table." Then Jesus answered her, "O woman, great is your faith! Be it done for you as you desire." And her daughter was healed instantly.

(Mat. 15:21-28; also Mk. 7:24-30)

The woman described by Mark as a Greek from Syro-Phoenicia is called a Canaanite by Matthew in order to make her seem as alien as possible. Matthew was concerned that Mark gave the impression all gentiles had equal rights with Jews to the ministry of Jesus. So when Matthew told stories about gentiles having faith, these gentiles had to always be unusual in having a special kind of faith in God. Matthew called her a Canaanite, making her a member of the most hated of all gentiles, those who seduced Israel from her faith in Yahweh.

The Canaanites were especially notorious among the Jews for their immoral worship rituals, often using temple prostitutes. Hebrew men were especially attracted to Canaanite women, probably because of their sexual sophistication. The Hebrew prophets railed more against Canaanite deities than against any others.

Matthew called her a Canaanite to stress that she was from a people who were regarded as the most dangerous of all Israel's enemies. For such a foreigner to have any faith at all in Israel's God was extraordinary. Matthew reinforced this by having Jesus say that her faith was great. In other words—and the same tactic was used by Matthew in the story of the healing of the Roman centurion's servant or son—

this gentile woman, although coming from the most unclean of all gentile nations, has a depth of faith greater than that of most Jews, and this made it possible for Jesus to heal her daughter. Thus, says the gospel of Matthew, you cannot use gentiles like her to prove the gospel was made available to all gentiles on the same basis as it was made available to the people of God.

It is interesting to note that when the gospel of Matthew was written, gentiles were pouring into the church and swamping the Christians who had once been Jews, resulting in these Christians losing leadership positions in the congregations. They believed that because they had been the first to come to Christ they should be first in line for leadership positions.

But what is important about this story, especially as told by Matthew, is the way this Canaanite woman went completely outside social convention, not only by daring to confront a Jewish male, but by taking over a responsibility her husband should have exercised. No doubt her husband was a true Canaanite and believed only in his gods, and was not prepared to forsake them in favor of the hated Jewish God. Had it been his son who was sick and he had been sure of Jesus' ability to heal him, maybe it would have been a different story. But I doubt he would have been able to abase himself to the Israelite as his wife did.

No doubt this woman took heart from the fact that this Jew, Jesus, had left his home territory, Galilee, and had come into her territory of Tyre and Sidon. He and his disciples were now the foreigners, the ones out of place. Jesus did not often leave Jewish territory. Matthew tells us that on this occasion he "withdrew," probably to get away from people who had been troubling him. Mark says he entered a house, which meant he had friends in this foreign country, and he did not want it known that he was there. But it was not to be.

The reaction of Jesus' disciples was also typical, "Send her away, for she is crying after us." How dare she, this gentile and a woman in the bargain, come unbidden before the Master and ask for what is the right only of the Jews? Women had no right to speak directly to male leaders, either about religion or politics; they had to ask their husband or father or brother or son or uncle to intercede on their behalf. Not only this, but she came into their space unbidden. There had been no welcome rituals—no acknowledgment that she was out of place in this space, especially in this space occupied by men only. She remained a stranger and a foreigner, daring to assert herself as both a woman and a foreigner in space that was sacred to men. In other words, she behaved like a prostitute.

But this outrageous woman was more concerned about the health of her daughter than about the social niceties of both the Jews and gentiles of her society, and demanded to be heard. She was more concerned about her daughter than about what these Jewish males might think of her. She knew what she was doing, and she dared them to do something about it.

Had Jesus not been there they, no doubt, would have walked away from her and ignored her. They could not physically touch her, for to do so would have been to make themselves ritually unclean—tainted by her out-of-placeness. As it was, they spoke about her to Jesus, and not directly to her. To even acknowledge her presence to her face would have given her a place in their space.

Jesus, not the disciples, heard her, and answered her call for healing her daughter. She was prepared to be seen as a whore and a social outcast rather than allow an opportunity for the healing of her daughter to pass by.

Jesus at first reinforced her position as being out of place. His place, as an Israelite, was among the people of Israel. He was committed to being their Messiah. Once he left Israel, he was out of place. For him to come to her daughter's aid was to make himself profane. His sacred duty was to Israel: any service to non-Israelites was a non-sacred service. She was asking him to step out of his place and enter her place and exchange his sacredness for hers.

But she persists: "Please, help me Lord!"

Jesus then made her situation sound even more bleak. "It is not fair to take the children's bread and throw it to the dogs."

If you had been that Canaanite mother, you would have recoiled at the stark contrast between the children of the household at the family table and the dogs waiting anxiously outside for the scraps.

Dogs were not kept as pets the way we in Western society keep them today. Dogs were usually ownerless, roaming the streets and lanes in packs, scrabbling around rubbish heaps and fighting at doorways during meal times for survival. All dogs were regarded as unclean — out of place in the household, unfit to be touched or handled, useful only for disposing of food scraps and bones. Dogs were thus pariahs — useless, apart from disposing of leftover food. The only exception were those dogs especially bred and trained for tending sheep and goats.

Jesus was likening her to a useless, unwelcome and unclean animal, roaming around the streets, trying to steal what really belonged to the children of the household! But she was undaunted. She knew householders used the dogs to get rid of unwanted scraps of food. "True, Lord; but even the dogs are thrown the scraps of food the children leave on the floor."

She was acknowledging what Jesus had put to her; she was out of place in Israel, Jesus' land, and had no right to demand from him what belonged only to his people. To qualify for Jesus' healing, she should first of all become a Jew, and then ask for her daughter to be made well. But she knew, and Jesus knew, that the only way she could become an Israelite was for her husband to convert. Remember, a woman's identity flowed from her husband's. The fact she was there and not her husband was sufficient indication that this was impossible.

She was not asking for a place in Israel. She was asking that, like the dogs who were tolerated but given no proper place in the household, she would be tolerated as a stranger and be thrown a scrap of unwanted bread. She just wanted her daughter to be healed by this Israelite man whom she knew was gifted as a healer.

What we see here is a very typical confrontation between two Mediterraneans: a male Israelite of some authority and reputation, and a Canaanite woman, out of place in Israelite territory with no social standing whatsoever.

By accepting her place as defined by Jesus and by asking to be treated as a stray she caused no trouble for Jesus. She accepted his gift of healing on his terms, even though she had asserted her right to make the first move. What had been a rather dangerous strategy for her turned out to benefit the one she most cared about — her sick daughter.

From Matthew's perspective in writing to assert the priority of Jews over gentiles in the church, her behavior and her faith in Jesus were so outstanding as to be atypical of gentiles, and therefore she could not be used as proof that Jesus welcomed all gentiles into the Messianic family.

Jesus finally gave her what her heart desired, making it clear that he could heal her daughter only because of her outstanding faith in him and because of her clear acknowledgment of her true place as a stranger with no rights to Israel's Messiah.

The Mother of James and John

Then the mother of the sons of Zebedee came up to him, with her sons, and kneeling before him she asked him for something. And he said to her, "What do you want?" She said to him, "Command that these two sons of mine may sit, one at your right hand and one at your left, in your kingdom." But Jesus answered, "You do not know what you are asking. Are you able to drink the cup that I am to drink?" They said to him, "We are able." He said to them, "You will drink my cup, but to sit at my right hand and at my left is not mine to grant, but it is for those for whom it has been pre-pared by my Father." And when the ten heard it, they were indignant at the two brothers.

(Mat. 20:20-24; also Mk. 10:35-41)

When James and John left home to join Jesus they had done a so-cially unacceptable thing: they had dishonored their father. Zebedee had a large family fishing business and would have been much honored in his village. His eldest son would have been expected to take over this business on his death and thus continue the honored position of the family in the community. He would have been expected to find husbands and dowries for any unmarried sisters and help any unmar-ried brothers set up their homes, as well as care for his wife and make sure she had adequate support should he die before she did. So when both sons left the business to follow Jesus, they would have been con-sidered irresponsible, bringing dishonor to their father. On Zebedee's death who would carry on the business and the family honor? The whole village would have been in utter turmoil over such behavior, and Zebedee would have been blamed for not having brought up his sons properly. The village would also have been upset that their whole reputation had been put at risk by the behavior of these young men.

Jewish men took their role as family head very seriously. The honor of the village with respect to other villages depended to a large extent on the maintenance of family honor by each of its families. The eldest son was not free to leave home and take up a trade or occupation different from his father's. Life choices were severely limited in a world perceived to be of limited resources.

So when these young men responded to the call of Jesus and left home they not only acted against the will of their father and the expectations of their village, they also brought upon the family name and the village reputation a great amount of dishonor and shame.

Two years later, Jesus was being honored as the Messiah who would soon cast off the yoke of the Roman invaders and restore honor to Israel. Zebedee had gone to his grave in dishonor. This must have been the case, for otherwise there is no way his wife would have dared to come unbidden before Jesus.

Zebedee's widow decided to do something about restoring honor to her late husband's name. Notice she is not named, simply referred to as the wife of this well-known fishing entrepreneur. The identity of a wife was embedded in that of her husband, even though he had died. She went to Jesus, unbidden, knelt before him like a slave—an action outlandish for a woman who was once honored as the wife of Zebedee—and asked that her two sons be made the Messiah's chief assistants in the coming kingdom.

Bear in mind that this happened in public, somewhere out in the open where a great number of people would have seen it. This was not behind closed doors nor in a foreign country, as in the case of the Canaanite woman. And rightly so: this widow had been publicly shamed by her sons leaving home, and now she wanted to regain that honor just as publicly.

But once again she had stepped out of her place. Her place was in her home, looking after the household and making sure it ran smoothly. She could legitimately move outside her place only to do the shopping and perhaps take some food to a needy neighbor.

Her action of publicly kneeling before Jesus was her way of acknowledging that she was out of place. For her to have stood in Jesus'
presence would have been considered the act of a person who believed
she had social equality with Jesus. For a woman that would have
been doubly shameful: women waited to be asked before speaking to
a man; and no woman had any honorable position in society apart from
her male sponsor.

In asking for her sons to be Jesus' senior assistants she was trying to ensure that her sons would have positions of honor far in excess
of those they left behind when they joined Jesus. She wanted to be
able to go back to her village in triumph and announce to all that her
sons had acquired greater honor than they had left behind. Thus she
would regain—even enhance—her husband's lost honor. And since this
would have happened in public, there would have been plenty of male
witnesses to attest to her claim. Again, you need to remember that the
word of a Jewish woman had no standing at all in Jewish society;
everything had to be attested to by the support of male witnesses.

We must see her act in its social context. Although Jesus went on
to show how she was misguided, that in the kingdom of God honor
was not a factor in social relationships, he did not criticize her. He knew
her concern was not so much for herself but for the honor of her late
husband and her village.

In fact, both Matthew and Mark report how Jesus used her
shameful behavior to teach his disciples a rather important lesson in
honor and leadership. He showed how the male concepts of honor and
leadership that drove her to this action would not apply in the kingdom he would establish. True leaders will give up the honor that once
went with leadership and take on the social position of the most despised segment of the community—slaves. Leaders will serve like
slaves, not rule like lords and masters.

I find it interesting that Mark did not have her asking this of Jesus, but of the men themselves. Matthew, on the other hand, wanted
his men to come out squeaky clean, so burdens the woman with the
blame.

I admire this widowed mother. Her outrageous behavior on behalf of her family is deserving of far more recognition than it generally

finds. Without her, we might never have been given the leadership model Jesus enshrined for use by the church.

Anna the Prophet

> And there was a prophetess, Anna, the daughter of Phanuel, of the tribe of Asher; she was of a great age, having lived with her husband seven years from her virginity, and as a widow till she was eighty-four. She did not depart from the temple, worshiping with fasting and prayer night and day. And coming up at that very hour she gave thanks to God, and spoke of him to all who were looking for the redemption of Jerusalem.
>
> *(Lk. 2:36-38)*

When Jesus was presented to God in the temple after his circumcision, two people celebrated with Jesus and his parents. One was Simeon, a righteous and devout man who was praying earnestly for the salvation of Israel. God's Spirit revealed to him that Jesus was the Messiah, so he took the babe into his arms and prophesied in the words of the song we now call the "Nunc Dimittis."

An elderly woman was there and heard Simeon's prophesy. She was from the tribe of Asher, one of the few tribes that had responded to Hezekiah's call to revive the Passover at Jerusalem during a time when the nation was in disarray. She had married as a virgin and lived most of her adult life as a widow, now eighty-four. In those days, widows had to be supported by friends and family, for they would have been unable to earn money for themselves. Luke calls her a prophet. Judaism had no time for women as priests, prophets or queens. In the Old Testament most of the women associated with religion and government were evil.

Anna was too old to take in washing, even if she had been allowed to earn money for herself. But she was not too old to be a prophet. Having come to the temple for Jesus' presentation, "she gave thanks to God and spoke of him to all who were looking for the redemption of Jerusalem." When no one else in authority was proclaiming the birth of the Messiah, this old woman was telling the world.

How rebellious of her! Old women, it was thought, should sit at the back and get on with their prayers and not open their toothless mouths! Women of any age had no right to be saying anything, because no one would believe them until at least two males agreed with what they were saying. Anna knew no one would take much notice of her; but she also knew the inner urge of God's Spirit to proclaim the truth that had been given to her. She obeyed God, and that was all that mattered to her. She let people ignore her message at their own peril!

The Woman Who Celebrated Womanhood

Jesus had been challenged about his ability to cast out demons. There were those who scoffed at him, accusing him of being in league with the Devil. But he soon put them in their place by showing up the stupidity of any leader who would employ servants to undermine his own authority. Then a woman in the crowd astounded all around her by shouting out:

> Blessed is the womb that bore you, and the breasts that you sucked!
>
> *(Lk. 11:27)*

Here we have a very interesting situation. Jesus' enemies, most likely influential Pharisees, challenge him by trying to shame him in the presence of those he was teaching by accusing him of being in league with the Devil. But, as always, Jesus bested them in this game of challenge and response.

In such situations there would normally be some public acclamation to the victor. Mediterraneans took these games very seriously and liked nothing better than to crowd around and applaud the victor.

But who applauded Jesus in his victory over his would-be detractors? One solitary woman. And she should not have been seen, let alone heard since these were games only men took part in and observed.

Notice how she attributed the ultimate honor to the womb that bore him and the breasts that nurtured him. In a society where all the honor for begetting went to the male, this outburst was outrageous in the extreme, and would have earned her bitter castigations from the men surrounding her.

But what was Jesus' reply to her?

> Blessed rather are those who hear the word of God and keep it!
>
> *(Lk. 11:28)*

Notice that Jesus did not rebuke her, as the crowd would have expected. His use here of "rather," the only time this word is used in the New Testament, is not to deny her statement that his mother was blessed in giving him birth. Indeed in Luke's gospel, the birth of Jesus is a blessed event and Mary is declared to be "blessed" by her cousin Elizabeth: "Blessed are you among women and blessed is the fruit of your womb!" (Lk. 1:42)

What Jesus was saying here was: "You are quite right. God did bless my mother in giving birth to me. But you must not attribute to her my power to cast out demons. The only people who are given God's power to do anything good are those who hear the words God utters and carry them out in their lives."

Thus does Jesus use the temerity of an anonymous woman to make a most important point.

The Maid Who Challenged Peter

Then they seized him and led him away, bringing him into the high priest's house. Peter followed at a distance; and when they had kindled a fire in the middle of the courtyard and sat down together, Peter sat among them. Then a maid, seeing him as he sat in the light and gazing at him, said, "This man also was with him." But he denied it, saying, "Woman, I do not know him." And a little later someone else saw him and said, "You also are one of them." But Peter said, "Man, I am not." And after an interval of about an hour still another insisted, saying, "Certainly this man also was with him; for he is a Galilean." But Peter said, "Man, I do not know what you are saying." And immediately, while he was still speaking, the cock crowed.

(Lk. 22:54-60; also Mat. 26:69-75 and Jn. 18:16-18)

She was a saucy one, the young slave girl whose job it was to see that visitors doffed their dusty sandals before they entered the high priest's house, washed their feet and made sure they brought no out-of-place dust inside. She stepped completely out of line when she strode up to Peter and accused him of being in league with the traitor Jesus.

Since Peter was out of place in the courtyard of this high priest's house and had come in unbidden, she probably felt it was worth the risk. She would not have dared to behave in this way to any there who had been invited. But she actually started quite a trend, for soon afterward a couple of men took up the challenge and accused him of being a traitor to Israel.

I wonder whether any of those men would have bothered had this young girl not behaved so outrageously toward a man who may or may not have been a guest of the high priest?

Peter ended up convicting himself of lying and betraying the very master whom he had sworn to follow to the death!

When leaders are allowed to get away with corrupt leadership, it often falls to the lot of outspoken women to tell the truth, no matter what their station in life. And this woman made no pretense whatsoever of being religious. Notice also that once she had taken such a bold step, two men followed her and challenged Peter, resulting in his final downfall and the acknowledgment of his denial of Jesus.

The Samaritan Woman at the Well

Now when the Lord knew that the Pharisees had heard that Jesus was making and baptizing more disciples than John (although Jesus himself did not baptize, but only his disciples), he left Judea and departed again to Galilee. He had to pass through Samaria. So he came to a city of Samaria, called Sychar, near the field that Jacob gave to his son Joseph. Jacob's well was there, and so Jesus, wearied as he was with his journey, sat down beside the well. It was about the sixth hour.

There came a woman of Samaria to draw water. Jesus said to her, "Give me a drink." For his disciples had gone away into the city to buy food. The Samaritan woman said to him, "How is it that you, a Jew, ask a drink of me, a woman of Samaria?" For Jews have no dealings with Samaritans. Jesus answered her, "If you knew the gift of God, and who it is that is saying to you, 'Give me a drink,' you would have asked him, and he would have given you living water." The woman said to him, "Sir, you have nothing to draw with, and the well is deep; where do you get that living water? Are you greater than our father Jacob, who gave us the well, and drank from it himself, and his sons, and his cattle?" Jesus said to her, "Every one who drinks of this water will thirst again, but whoever drinks of the water that I shall give him will never thirst; the water that I shall give him will become in him a spring of water welling up to eternal life." The woman said to him, "Sir, give me this water, that I may not thirst, nor come here to draw."

Jesus said to her, "Go, call your husband, and come here." The woman answered him, "I have no husband." Jesus said to her, "You are right in saying, 'I have no husband'; for you have had five husbands, and he whom you now have is not your husband; this you said truly." The woman said to him, "Sir, I perceive that you are a prophet. Our fathers worshiped on this mountain; and you say that in Jerusalem is the place where men ought to worship." Jesus said to her, "Woman, believe me, the hour is coming when neither on this mountain nor in Jerusalem will you worship the Father. You worship what you do not know; we worship what we know, for salvation is from the Jews. But the hour is coming, and now is, when the true worshipers will worship the Father in spirit and truth, for such the Father seeks to worship him. God is spirit, and those who worship him must worship in spirit and truth." The woman said to him, "I know that Messiah is coming (he who is called Christ); when he comes, he will show us all things." Jesus said to her, "I who speak to you am he." Just then his disciples came. They marveled that he was talking with a woman, but none said, "What do you wish?" or, "Why are you talking with her?" So the woman left her water jar, and went away into the city, and said to the people, "Come, see a man who told me all that I ever did. Can this be the Christ?" They went out of the city and were coming to him.

Meanwhile the disciples besought him, saying, "Rabbi, eat." But he said to them, "I have food to eat of which you do not know." So the disciples said to one another, "Has any one brought him food?" Jesus said to them, "My food is to do the will of him who sent me, and to accomplish his work. Do you not say, 'There are yet four months, then comes the harvest'? I tell you, lift up your eyes, and see how the fields are already white for harvest. He who reaps receives wages, and gathers fruit for eternal life, so that sower and reaper may rejoice together. For here the saying holds true,

'One sows and another reaps.' I sent you to reap that for which you did not labor; others have labored, and you have entered into their labor."

Many Samaritans from that city believed in him because of the woman's testimony, "He told me all that I ever did." So when the Samaritans came to him, they asked him to stay with them; and he stayed there two days. And many more believed because of his word. They said to the woman, "It is no longer because of your words that we believe, for we have heard for ourselves, and we know that this is indeed the Savior of the world."

(Jn. 4:1-42)

This woman had everything against her. She was a Samaritan. No Jewish male would dare to be seen talking to a Samaritan man, let alone a woman. Samaritans, you see, had betrayed the true faith of Israel by marrying foreign women and setting up their own temple on Mt. Gerizim. And she was also a bad woman; she had five husbands — fortunately for her not all at the same time — and was now living in sin with a sixth man. This was why she came in the middle of the day to collect water from the village well, knowing there would be no other women there to accuse her of being a sinner.

Jesus was once again out of place in foreign territory. This was Samaria, and Jews avoided Samaria like the plague. When Jesus arrived at the well, he must have known why she was there at that time of the day. Indeed we know that because he talked about her having had five husbands.

When he asked her for some water, she quite outrageously criticized him for daring to talk to her since he knew she was a Samaritan. Had she behaved as befitted any woman in such circumstances, she would not have made any reply to this person — a male, a foreigner. She would simply have acceded to his request and given him a drink of water. But she was an outcast in her own village, and she probably felt she had nothing more to lose, so she gave vent to her feelings.

Soon she and Jesus were engaged in some rather heavy theology, until she finally realized he must be the true Messiah. It is interesting to read John's account of this conversation and to notice how well she had listened to the men in her life when they discussed religious issues.

She would not have been allowed to do more than listen since women were discouraged from taking an interest in the faith. Yet she could say to Jesus, "I know the Messiah is coming and he will show us all things."

When Jesus told her he was the Messiah she tore back to her village, risked the ire and jeering of the people, and shouted to all that she had just been talking with the Messiah. That whole village turned to their Messiah that day, and all because an outrageous woman demanded to be heard, both by the Messiah and by the village that despised her.

But notice how in the end the Samaritan men downplayed her part in their recognition of Jesus as Messiah: "It is no longer because of your words that we believe, for we have heard for ourselves, and we know that this is indeed the Savior of the world." This is a reminder that in a Jewish court the testimony of a woman needed the corroborative testimony of several men before it could be accepted. (Court cases in our own day involving battered wives remind us that little has changed.)

These six women are typical of the way some women stood outside their social position in a male dominated society and demanded to be listened to. They had needs too; they had important things to say; they helped run the family and the village and were prepared to go directly to Jesus with a sure instinct that he would most certainly listen to them and give them a chance.

In each case they were rewarded with their request answered or their message heard.

The Women Who Mourned on the Way to the Cross

After Pilate condemned Jesus to death by crucifixion, the soldiers led him away. A huge crowd of bystanders immediately joined in the procession, including some women who raised their voices in mourning for a Messiah who held out so much hope for their freedom from the social, political and religious oppression that characterized their everyday lives.

If you have ever watched Middle-Eastern or Bosnian women mourning the loss of their loved ones in war, you'll have some idea of the loudness of the sound they made. No one could possibly ignore them.

> And as they led him away, they seized one Simon of Cyrene, who was coming in from the country, and laid on him the cross, to carry it behind Jesus. And there followed him a great multitude of the people, and of women who bewailed and lamented him. But Jesus turning to them said, "Daughters of Jerusalem, do not weep for me, but weep for yourselves and for your children. For behold, the days are coming when they will say, 'Blessed are the barren, and the wombs that never bore, and the breasts that never gave suck!' Then they will begin to say to the mountains, 'Fall on us' and to the hills, 'Cover us.' For if they do this when the wood is green, what will happen when it is dry?"
>
> *(Lk. 23:26-31)*

The beating of their breast and their loud ululations, together with the tearing of their outer garments and urgent petitions to Yahweh for mercy—all these were expected of women at the death of any of their menfolk.

But that these women would dare to make such public expressions of mourning and grief over a man condemned to death by both church and state was rebellious in the extreme. I have no doubt the temple leaders, as well as the Roman guard, would have done their best to shut them up.

Jesus, in the midst of his own personal pain and fear at the coming torture of crucifixion, stopped them in his tracks and virtually thanked them for considering him one of their kin. He called them "daughters of Jerusalem." Did he call any male there "a son of Jerusalem"? Jerusalem was the city of David and, in prophecy, the center of God's presence in the world. He was thus calling them "Yahweh's daughters"!

And then he went on to warn that their future would be far worse than his. From being the breeders and nurturers of children, they would become machines for the selfish satisfaction of males. Their bodies, designed by Yahweh for love and nurture, would become the tools and objects for male domination.

I have no doubt that these wonderful women, protesting at a great injustice perpetrated by the dominant males of their society, now continued in silence, mourning inwardly and by outward gestures for the son of Mary. Theirs was the first act of civil disobedience in Christian history.

And where were the eleven male disciples? Were they somewhere in that procession? It seems not. Only John appeared during the crucifixion.

So, here we have this great number of anonymous women appearing out of nowhere, yet seeming to know who Jesus was and what he would have done for their lives had he lived to head up the new kingdom of God.

And they had no hesitation in breaking the rules of public social mores to declare their opposition to this great injustice being perpetrated on their champion.

Demanding the Right to be Ministered To

The next group of women represent those who came to Jesus with personal needs. The previous group came with requests for others. But this group of women had to step even more out of line, for only their male sponsors had any right to make requests on their behalf.

The Woman with the Issue of Blood

And a woman who had had a flow of blood for twelve years and could not be healed by anyone, came up behind him, and touched the fringe of his garment; and immediately her flow of blood ceased. And Jesus said, "Who was it that touched me?" When all denied it, Peter said, "Master, the multitudes surround you and press upon you!" But Jesus said, "Some one touched me; for I perceive that power has gone forth from me." And when the woman saw that she was not hidden, she came trembling, and falling down before him declared in the presence of all the people why she had touched him, and how she had been immediately healed.

And he said to her, "Daughter, your faith has made you well; go in peace."

(Lk. 8:43-48; also Mat. 9:20-22 and Mk. 5:25-34)

This woman was caught in a no-win situation. Any person, male or female, who was suffering from an illness that resulted in emission of fluids of any kind from the body was labeled "unclean" and was not allowed to make social contact with other people and was especially forbidden to attend worship in the synagogue and temple. Body fluids were considered out of place and had to be dealt with to avoid risk to the good order of the community. There were elaborate rituals that had to be done in the sight of the family—washings and reclothing—before normal social mixing was possible.

All societies define what is safe for their members and in the process devise ways of protecting themselves from those who act outside the safety rules. In the Jewish society of Jesus' day, only a person with a whole body was a completely safe person with whom others could relate. A man with crushed testicles or a missing hand, for example, was not allowed to serve in the temple or synagogue.

All emission of fluids from any part of the body rendered a person a danger to the welfare of the community. Such persons had to be marked and excluded: they were thus labeled "unclean," primarily for religious and political reasons. A husband and wife engaging in sexual intercourse were doing a perfectly normal and natural thing. But because semen had been emitted from his body into hers, both were in an unsafe condition. This was corrected by having a bath as soon as possible afterward, thus making them safe to mix with the rest of the community. (I have often pictured the Israelite men wandering in the wilderness for forty years debating the worthwhileness of making love to their wives when they had to spend so much of their physical energy lugging enough water around the desert to make such activity possible!)

It was because Jews could not be too sure about how gentiles dealt with emissions of bodily fluid that they labeled all gentiles unclean. Public washing and reclothing were required of any gentiles who wished to become members of a Jewish community. In the case of men, this also involved their undergoing circumcision.

I've gone into some detail about this so you can see just how outrageous the behavior of the woman was with the issue of blood. We tend to think of her as having some kind of continual menstruation, whereas the blood could have been coming from anywhere in her body. It could have resulted from an ulcer that continually exuded blood. This continuous emission of blood meant she could not sleep with her husband, if she had one; could not cook for her children, if she had any; could not go shopping; she could not go to the synagogue and temple to ask God for healing. She was in a state of total alienation from her family, the community, and from God.

When this nameless woman forced her way through the crowds following Jesus to the house of Jairus, leader of the synagogue, and dared to touch Jesus' garment, she was breaking every social convention. She would have been well-known. Certainly Jairus would have known her because it was his responsibility to see that such people did not gain entrance to the synagogue. Every person in that crowd she touched would have been made unclean, and when she touched Jesus she made him unclean for seven days.

Her behavior was outrageous in the extreme. But she was desperate. No physicians had been able to help her over the years. She could not gain access to priests or healers in the temple. Only Jesus could bring her back into the community. And she dared the wrath of the community, who could well have lynched her in its anger at such temerity.

But notice Jesus' attitude. He did not once challenge her for breaking social convention. He did not once condemn her for making him unclean and therefore unfit to go ahead and heal Jairus' daughter.

What he did was to force her to identify herself publicly before the crowd. He then confirmed she no longer had this emission of blood. "Go in peace" is very expressive here, for it says to all around that no uncleanness had been imparted to anyone, not even to himself. The community was healed and made whole too. Both she and everyone she had brushed against were restored to social and religious safety.

He had felt healing power flow out of his body and into hers. This process ensured that social norms were irrelevant—even dehumanizing. The healing power of God bows to no human convention when the life and well-being of a single believer is threatened.

The behavior of this woman is a sign to us that the exclusion of women from equal fellowship in the church will be met with rebellious reactions of women as they struggle for recognition and equality. Too often we force people to behave in ways we label "selfish," when all the time we are marginalizing them and forcing them to take actions we call "antisocial."

Mary and Martha the Sisters of Lazarus

Now as they went on their way, he entered a village; and a woman named Martha received him into her house. And she had a sister called Mary, who sat at the Lord's feet and listened to his teaching. But Martha was distracted with much serving; and she went to him and said, "Lord, do you not care that my sister has left me to serve alone? Tell her then to help me." But the Lord answered her, "Martha, Martha, you are anxious and troubled about many things; one thing is needful. Mary has chosen the good portion, which shall not be taken away from her."

(Lk. 10:38-42)

Jesus did an outrageous thing: he went into a house where he would be alone with two unmarried women! That was taboo among Jews in those days. Two men could be alone in a house with one woman, but not the other way around. That's how much men feared the sexual power of women! (Doesn't it remind you of some of the rhetoric of the men who shudder at the idea of a woman at the altar and in the pulpit and what thoughts she will engender in the minds of the men in the pews?)

But there Jesus was in the small village of Bethany, alone in the house with Martha and Mary. Everyone in the village would have seen him go in. Knowing Lazarus, their brother, was away on business, the curious would find some excuse to go walking past the house and gaze in through window and door to see what might be going on inside.

Any decent woman would have asked him to leave and return when Lazarus was back, or at least have stayed on her feet so as to make it quite clear nothing untoward was going on. But no. Look at Mary. She sat herself down on the floor at Jesus' feet and listened attentively while he taught her.

No wonder Martha panicked. She tore around the house making as much noise as she could to distract the neighbors, hoping her stupid sister would get the message and get on her feet and save their reputation!

But no. She stayed there.

Finally, Martha could bear it no longer and scolded Jesus for allowing them to be in this awkward situation. She didn't really care at all about the housework that needed doing—she had probably washed the dishes four times by then! But she did care about the reputation of her family. Jesus knew what was really troubling her and did not take her implied criticism of himself unkindly. After all it was he who had breached the social etiquette.

"Martha, Martha! Calm down! Forget about these stupid social niceties! It is more important to understand the truths of the kingdom than it is to know which way to spoon out your soup!

"Mary can't concentrate on listening to me while doing things the way you can. She needs to give me her full attention in order to learn from me. You can listen and do the housework at the same time. I don't care which way you listen, as long as you listen and learn and carry out what I teach you. I'm certainly not going to force Mary to listen with only half an ear because you worry too much about what people will think."

Both the women were rebellious in their own way. Martha in not asking Jesus to leave, and Mary in risking her reputation and her sister's by sitting quietly at his feet.

There are times when social niceties have to be discarded, when people's lives and souls are more at risk by keeping to society's rules.

Martha and Mary Again

Now a certain man was ill, Lazarus of Bethany, in the village of Mary and her sister Martha. It was Mary, who anointed the Lord with ointment and wiped his feet with her hair, whose brother Lazarus was ill. So the sisters sent to him, saying, "Lord, he whom you love is ill." But when Jesus heard it he said, "This illness is not unto death; it is for the glory of God, so that the Son of God may be glorified by means of it."

Now Jesus loved Martha and her sister and Lazarus. So when he heard that he was ill, he stayed two days longer in the place where he was. Then after this he said to the disciples, "Let us go into Judea again." The disciples said to him, "Rabbi, the Jews were but now seeking to stone you, and are you going there again?" Jesus answered, "Are there not twelve hours in the day? If any one walks in the day, he does not stumble, because he sees the light of this world. But if anyone walks in the night, he stumbles, because the light is not in him." Thus he spoke, and then he said to them, "Our friend Lazarus has fallen asleep, but I go to awake him out of sleep." The disciples said to him, "Lord, if he has fallen asleep, he will recover." Now Jesus had spoken of his death, but they thought that he meant taking rest in sleep. Then Jesus told them plainly, "Lazarus is dead; and for your sake I am glad that I was not there, so that you may believe. But let us go to him." Thomas, called the Twin, said to his fellow disciples, "Let us also go, that we may die with him."

Now when Jesus came, he found that Lazarus had already been in the tomb four days. Bethany was near Jerusalem, about two miles off, and many of the Jews had come to Martha and Mary to console them concerning their brother. When Martha heard that Jesus was coming, she went and met him, while Mary sat in the house. Martha said to Jesus, "Lord, if you had been here, my brother would not have died. And even now I know that whatever you ask from God, God will give you." Jesus said to her, "Your brother will rise again." Martha said to him, "I know that he will rise again in the resurrection at the last day." Jesus said to her, "I am the resurrection and the life; he who believes in me, though he die, yet shall he live, and whoever lives and believes in me shall never die. Do you believe this?" She said to him, "Yes, Lord; I believe that you are the Christ, the Son of God, he who is coming into the world."

When she had said this, she went and called her sister Mary, saying quietly, "The Teacher is here and is calling for you." And when she heard it, she rose quickly and went to him. Now Jesus had not yet come to the village, but was still in the place where Martha had met him. When the Jews who were with her in the house, consoling her, saw Mary rise quickly and go out, they followed her, supposing that she was going to the tomb to weep there. Then Mary, when she came where Jesus was and saw him, fell at his feet, saying to him, "Lord, if you had been here, my brother would not have died." When Jesus saw her weeping, and the Jews who came with her also weeping, he was deeply moved in spirit and troubled; and he said, "Where have you laid him?" They said to him, "Lord, come and see." Jesus wept. So the Jews said, "See how he loved him!" But some of them said, "Could not he who opened the eyes of the blind man have kept this man from dying?"

Then Jesus, deeply moved again, came to the tomb; it was a cave, and a stone lay upon it. Jesus said, "Take away the stone." Martha, the sister of the dead man, said to him, "Lord, by this time there will be an odor, for he has been dead four days." Jesus said to her, "Did I not tell you that if you would believe you would see the glory of God?" So they took away the stone. And Jesus lifted up his eyes and said, "Father, I thank thee that thou hast heard me. I knew that thou hearest me always, but I have said this on account of the people standing by, that they may believe that thou didst send me." When he had said this, he cried with a loud voice, "Lazarus, come out." The dead man came out, his hands and feet bound with bandages, and his face wrapped with a cloth. Jesus said to them, "Unbind him, and let him go." Many of the Jews therefore, who had come with Mary and had seen what he did, believed in him.

(Jn. 11:1-45)

Their brother Lazarus, their breadwinner, was seriously ill. Martha and Mary sent a message to Jesus asking him to come and heal him. But Jesus delayed and Lazarus died.

Martha, the older sister, came out to meet Jesus, leaving Mary in the house. Lazarus has already been buried.

"Lord, if you had been here our brother would not have died."

I remind you here that women without men found it almost impossible to exist in that society. Any woman who took in washing or did some form of work was not paid directly. The money was given to her male sponsor: a husband or a son or a father or an uncle. Unattached women were an embarrassment in the ancient world. You have to read the passage about widows in I Timothy 5 in light of the fact that these young widows, if not members of an extended family, had only one way they could support themselves directly—prostitution. With no man to accept the wages of her labor, a single, unattached woman was not able to keep herself.

Martha and Mary were now in this predicament. Without their brother they could not earn their own living, keep their house and social respect.

Jesus raised Lazarus to life for their sake, not for his: after all, Lazarus was far better off in Abraham's bosom, was he not?

Martha's rebuke of Jesus was outrageous, even if true. She tempered this rebuke with the hope that Jesus would restore their brother to them. "Lord, if you had been here, my brother would not have died. And even now I know that whatever you ask from God, God will give you." She knew she and her family had a special relationship with Jesus that allowed her to express herself in this way, even in public. But there would have been many onlookers who would have gasped, her outspokenness being regarded as not proper for any decent woman.

She then returned home and sent Mary to Jesus. Mary greeted Jesus with the same rebuke, "If you had been here our brother would not have died." And she wept openly.

John states clearly that all the community gathered there were weeping too. They wept for the two women who now faced the rest of their lives manless and entirely dependent on the generosity of their village.

Martha's confession: "I believe that you are the Christ, the Son of God," is in itself an outrageous statement, since what women believed was of no value at all in that society.

But from their outrageousness came the miracle of the resurrection of Lazarus and the famous statement, "I am the resurrection and the life."

When Lazarus emerged from the tomb, still bound with the grave clothes soaked in ointment and precious balm, Jesus commanded that these bonds be removed. It would have been his sisters who would have done that, and given him a robe to wear until he reached their home.

This family was again reunited, the two sisters safe in the sponsorship of their brother, free to take up their roles in the life of their village.

It was during this incident that Jesus himself shed tears—the only time he did so. Those tears were in response to the tears of the two sisters who, in their own way, were appealing to him to help them escape a life of bitterness, poverty and shame. Their faith in him was not misplaced, just as the faith of all women who need to be rescued from social structures that oppress and punish them for being women will not be misplaced.

Martha and Mary a Third Time

Six days before the Passover, Jesus came to Bethany, where Lazarus was, whom Jesus had raised from the dead. There they made him a supper; Martha served, and Lazarus was one of those at table with him. Mary took a pound of costly ointment of pure nard and anointed the feet of Jesus and wiped his feet with her hair; and the house was filled with the fragrance of the ointment. But Judas Iscariot, one of his disciples (he who was to betray him), said, "Why was this ointment not sold for three hundred denarii and given to the poor?" This he said, not that he cared for the poor but because he was a thief, and as he had the money box he used to take what was put into it. Jesus said, "Let her alone, let her keep it for the day of my burial. The poor you always have with you, but you do not always have me."

(Jn. 12:1-8)

After the raising of Lazarus from the grave, Martha and Mary wanted to do something to express their heartfelt thanks at having their life and their brother given back to them. So they decided to give Jesus a feast. But it would have been Lazarus who issued the actual invitation. Martha served. There was, no doubt, a whole day of preparation for this feast. We can only imagine what food would have been served. Both sisters would have spent the day in excited preparation, putting their love into this meal.

John does not tell us about any guests being invited except the twelve disciples. Jesus reclined next to Lazarus, the head of the household. This places him at the seat of honor, rather different from the lowest place that was to be given when he went to the house of Simon the Pharisee, as you will see. In this case, Jesus would have been given the correct greeting, with his sandals taken off, his feet washed and his hair anointed with a sweet-smelling oil.

But during the meal, Mary came in. She would not have been seated with the men but instead would have been out in the kitchen helping Martha. Only Martha actually came into the dining area to serve the men. There would have been fourteen all told—Jesus, Lazarus and the twelve disciples.

Mary brought in some very expensive ointment of pure nard and anointed Jesus' feet, wiping it evenly over them with her long hair. The house filled with the exotic fragrance. That Mary would come in uninvited and perform this ritual was really outrageous, even in this family.

The reaction of Judas Iscariot, Jesus' ultimate betrayer, was predictable. He had assumed control of the finances of Jesus' mission, and apparently siphoned some of it off into his own pocket. It was inevitable he would miss the significance of Mary's action and think only of what he saw as a waste of money: the ultimate economic rationalist!

But Jesus was not going to be sidetracked. He appreciated Mary's gesture. She had sat at Jesus' feet some weeks earlier and had listened as he taught her about the coming kingdom of God and his part in it. Her response in anointing his feet—symbol of action and purpose—was an affirmation that she really did believe he was "the resurrection and the life." Once resurrected from the grave he would need his feet to move around his new kingdom. Jesus went on to tell Judas she must be allowed to keep the left-over ointment so she could anoint the rest of his body after his death.

Martha and Mary once again demonstrated that Jesus was happy with women who maintained their traditional roles—as Martha did—and with those who believed they should step out and make their own personal statement of faith—as Mary did.

The Crippled Woman

Now he was teaching in one of the synagogues on the Sabbath. And there was a woman who had had a spirit of infirmity for eighteen years; she was bent over and could not fully straighten herself. And when Jesus saw her, he called her and said to her, "Woman, you are freed from your infirmity." And he laid his hands upon her, and immediately she was made straight, and she praised God. But the ruler of the synagogue, indignant because Jesus had healed on the Sabbath, said to the people, "There are six days on which work ought to be done; come on those days and be healed, and not on the Sabbath day." Then the Lord answered him, "You hypocrites! Does not each of you on the Sabbath untie his ox or his ass from the manger, and lead it away to water it? And ought not this woman, a daughter of Abraham whom Satan bound for eighteen years, be loosed from this bond on the Sabbath day?" As he said this, all his adversaries were put to shame; and all the people rejoiced at all the glorious things that were done by him.

(Lk. 13:10-17)

This woman had been bent over double for eighteen years. Luke called this condition "a spirit of infirmity," indicating the community regarded her as demon-possessed. This meant she was ineligible to attend the temple and the synagogue. No one, man or woman, with any physical disability was supposed to appear before the Lord in public worship.

When Luke indicated Jesus "saw her" he probably meant she used to hide herself among the women in the gallery or at the back of the synagogue where women were isolated from the men. She needed to be careful that the leader of the synagogue did not see her, for he would have had her removed. Jesus thus deliberately went looking for her, knowing she was there.

He called out to her while he was teaching from the Scripture, "Woman, you are freed from your infirmity!" This sudden outburst was bad enough. That he would speak directly to a woman, and a crippled woman who had no right to be there in the first place, was bad enough. But that he broke the Sabbath law by performing the work of a healer by casting out her spirit of infirmity was the limit! The synagogue head made the assumption that Jesus was a professional healer, and therefore his act of healing was work and thus a breach of Sabbath law.

No wonder the ruler of the synagogue was upset. But he was not eager to criticize Jesus, you notice. He turned to the congregation, berated them, told them to come on the weekdays and not on the Sabbath if they wanted to be healed. He was primarily upset he had not seen this woman sneak in, and suspected some men in the congregation had helped her. This meant there were times during the week when those with disabilities could come and seek help from healers, but not on the Sabbath during worship. There would have been no other buildings in the towns where healers could have been sought out for consultation.

Jesus soon ended the argument by pointing out that every man present untied his ox or ass to take it out to water it on the Sabbath as on every other day—and isn't that doing work? He then called her "a daughter of Abraham." They had all regarded her as shameful because of her demon possession. They would never have referred to her as the wife of or the daughter of some man because to do so was to bring shame to the man named. But Jesus named Abraham as her father, thus removing any notion of shame from her. He not only healed her, but he removed her shame in the eyes of the community; he was also declaring her right to be there among them in their synagogue.

Her being in the synagogue during a Sabbath service was outrageous in the extreme; but the woman knew her rights before God.

Luke added a wonderful touch to end this story. "All his adversaries were put to shame; and all the people rejoiced at all the glorious things that were done by him."

These four women represent the women who believed they had the right to call upon Jesus for help to overcome personal problems and sickness. They believed Jesus would not take any notice of the social conventions that marginalized them and prevented them from taking steps to help themselves.

When men fail in their duty to help the very people they have made second-class citizens, sometimes those women need to go public and risk the ire of their menfolk in order to find the healing and peace they know has been promised them by God.

Demanding the Right to Serve

Women were generally not permitted to take up leadership roles in the community. Their roles were carefully defined as being within the household. There they did have some autonomy over household budgets, the cooking and housekeeping, and the care of young children. But when it came to service to the community, only men were allowed the right and privilege. Any public service performed by women had to be channeled through their men, which brought acknowledgment only to men.

The following examples show Jesus approving those women who chose to serve in their own right.

The Indigent Widow

And he sat down opposite the treasury, and watched the multitude putting money into the treasury. Many rich people put in large sums. And a poor widow came, and put in two copper coins, which make a penny. And he called his disciples to him, and said to them, "Truly, I say to you, this poor widow has put in more than all those who are contributing to the treasury. For they all contributed out of their abundance; but she out of her poverty has put in everything she had, her whole living."

(Mk. 12:41-44 and Lk. 21:1-4)

The Jews did not allow into the temple anything that had any kind of representation of a human form. Gentile money was automatically excluded because it always carried the head of the reigning Caesar and often the head of a pagan god.

Because only Roman and Greek coins were legal tender in the marketplace, the Jews were allowed to mint their own money for use within the temple. Only Jewish money could be used for offerings to God. These coins had no representation of humans or deities on them. To accommodate the need for worshipers to exchange their Roman money into temple money, the temple authorities set up money exchange booths at the entrance to the temple. Thus worshipers could bring their offerings in Roman money and exchange them for temple money at the door. This was, by the way, a lucrative business for the high priests who alone licensed these money dealers.

The widow who put two copper coins into the treasury—a large chest set up at the entrance so all could display how much they were giving to the temple—was acting quite outrageously on two accounts: she dared to put in such a small amount and think God would be pleased; and she dared to put in Roman money!

These copper coins the gospels mention were of such a small denomination that it was impractical for the Jews to mint equivalent temple money. So she was not able to exchange these two *lepta*. Since this was all she had, she placed them in the treasury as her offering to God.

This act would have stunned all the onlookers, especially the treasurer when he came to empty the box and count the coins. Watching the rich and famous openly flash the money they were putting into the treasury box was a popular pastime on Sabbath days. But Jesus commended her outrageousness: "She has put in more than all those who are contributing to the treasury."

Not only did this widow put in all she had in the world; she put in what was unacceptable to the men who ran the temple.

The Woman Who Anointed Jesus

Now when Jesus was at Bethany in the house of Simon the leper, a woman came up to him with an alabaster flask of very expensive ointment, and she poured it on his head, as he sat at table. But when the disciples saw it, they were indignant, saying, "Why this waste? For this ointment might have been sold for a large sum, and given to the poor." But Jesus, aware of this, said to them, "Why do you trouble the woman? For she has done a beautiful thing to me. For you always have the poor with you, but you will not always have me. In pouring this ointment on my body she has done it to prepare me for burial. Truly, I say to you, wherever this gospel is preached in the whole world, what she has done will be told in memory of her."

(Mat. 26:6-13 and Mk. 14:3-9)

The woman who gate-crashed a feast and anointed Jesus with costly ointment was probably a different one from the Mary of John's gospel who did the same thing, and from the unnamed woman who also gate-crashed a feast, but in the house of Simon the Pharisee. But the rebelliousness of the action was the same.

Picture the scene.

The village is Bethany, a rather small community where everyone knows everyone else's business. Jesus has been invited to a meal in the house of Simon the leper, so named because he was the Simon who had been cured of his leprosy.

There they were—all the men reclining on couches set around the walls, feasting away as the slave women served them and wiped their faces, picked up their discarded scraps and kept their chalices full of wine mixed with water. All the doors and windows were wide open so the entire village could see how sumptuously Jesus was being entertained.

And then a hush.

This unnamed woman comes boldly through the open front door, goes straight to where Jesus is reclining, kneels down at his feet, breaks open a cask of expensive ointment, pours it over Jesus' head and feet, and smooths it out with her long unbraided hair while weeping.

A couple of Jesus' disciples are angry at the dishonor this woman has brought to their master. They dare not voice their real feelings since this would be seen as a criticism of their master, so they blurt out something about such sinful waste of money that could have been used to feed the poor. What hypocrisy! They had not given the poor a single thought before then!

And what did such behavior provoke from Jesus?

"Leave her be! You'll have plenty of time to think about the poor when I'm dead and gone. This woman is anointing my body to prepare me for my coming painful death. Long after all of you have been gone and forgotten, this woman's brave and unselfish action will be celebrated."

This rebellious deed of a first-century woman demonstrates quite clearly that what matters is what is in the deepest hearts of women; for it is from the depths of the heart that one's true character emerges.

Yes, the motive and the deed may be rebellious, but God is able to see where they come from and responds justly and compassionately.

A Prostitute Who Anointed Jesus

One of the Pharisees asked him to eat with him, and he went into the Pharisee's house, and took his place at table. And behold, a woman of the city, who was a sinner, when she learned that he was at table in the Pharisee's house, brought an alabaster flask of ointment, and standing behind him at his feet, weeping, she began to wet his feet with her tears, and wiped them with the hair of her head, and kissed his feet, and anointed them with the ointment.

Now when the Pharisee who had invited him saw it, he said to himself, "If this man were a prophet, he would have known who and what sort of woman this is who is touching him, for she is a sinner." And Jesus answering said to him, "Simon, I have something to say to you." And he answered, "What is it, Teacher?" "A certain creditor had two debtors; one owed five hundred denarii, and the other fifty. When they could not pay, he forgave them both. Now which of them will love him more?" Simon answered, "The one, I suppose, to whom he forgave more."

And he said to him, "You have judged rightly." Then turning toward the woman he said to Simon, "Do you see this woman? I entered your house, you gave me no water for my feet, but she has wet my feet with her tears and wiped them with her hair. You gave me no kiss, but from the time I came in she has not ceased to kiss my feet. You did not anoint my head with oil, but she has anointed my feet with ointment. Therefore I tell you, her sins, which are many, are forgiven, for she loved much; but he who is forgiven little, loves little." And he said to her, "Your sins are forgiven." Then those who were at table with him began to say among themselves, "Who is this, who even forgives sins?" And he said to the woman, "Your faith has saved you; go in peace."

(Lk. 7:36-50)

This is certainly not the same woman who went to Simon the leper's house. Many of the circumstances are different. This story gives us an opportunity to look more closely at the place of women in the first century.

But first, what was Simon the Pharisee up to when he invited Jesus to a feast? Did he have a hidden agenda? Was he looking to make a fool of Jesus?

We need to have some idea of what went on at one of the main rituals used by upper class Jews as a way of maintaining their honor and status in their community.

In the first place, as I have already shown, only people perceived to be of equal status were invited to your house for a meal. These meals were part of the reciprocal relationships of the community: you invited only those who could invite you to their home in return, otherwise you would demean yourself by entering a lower-status house. To invite someone of a higher status than you was a risk, because that person might refuse and you would be publicly shamed.

Eating together implied shared ideals and values, and therefore where one sat, and who prepared what food in what utensils were of great concern to the community. There were two main stages to a formal meal. The first was conducted near the entrance to the house; one slave took off the dusty sandals of the guests and washed their feet in cool water, another anointed their heads with fragrant oil, while another one or two served the guests with appetizers.

After these initial ceremonies, the guests went to the dining room where they reclined in carefully placed order on couches on three sides of the room while being served their main meals. Scraps of bread were used to wipe the mouth and fingers and then thrown onto the floor for the slaves to gather up and give to the dogs that gathered at the door.

Everything had to be done perfectly to avoid adverse comment. The honor of the host was very much at stake here. Subjects for discussion were also carefully selected to minimize argumentation and preserve decorum. And, it goes without saying, only males were invited to such feasts. The women of the household would have been seen only when serving the guests, and stayed in the kitchen until called upon.

It was to such a feast that Simon the Pharisee invited Jesus.

At first glance, then, it would seem Simon the Pharisee recognized Jesus as being on an equal footing with himself. This could be assumed by the mere fact of the invitation. But as we read further we soon discover Jesus was not given the introductory courtesies. His feet were not washed and his head not anointed with oil. He was not even given the formal introductory kiss on the cheek normally given to all guests.

So—what were Simon's intentions?

There was, in fact, no way a rich Pharisee like Simon would have accepted Jesus as being of his own status. Jesus had been an artisan—

a carpenter—and therefore well down the social scale. Jesus had also dishonored his family by leaving his widowed mother and unmarried sisters to care for themselves.

The other guests Simon had invited would have been mortally offended at having such a person as Jesus reclining near them and would not have invited Simon to their home. Indeed, as soon as Jesus was spied, many would have walked off in a huff and thus shamed Simon.

What Simon did was to instruct his slaves to escort Jesus directly to his assigned place at the lowest end of the couches, thus signaling to the other guests that Jesus was to be an object of scorn. Simon and his guests would have been able to say what they wanted to Jesus without threatening their own status and honor. But, in fact, they would only do that if Jesus first drew attention to this lack of courtesy and asked why he had been treated so badly. This would then have opened the way for all the guests and Simon, as host, to assert their higher status.

These games of challenge and response were very craftily played in the community. You only took notice of someone of lower status when they first challenged you. To make the first move against someone below you was to risk losing the argument and being publicly shamed. If someone of lower status challenged you, you simply ignored the challenge and walked away, thus showing your superiority.

In this situation, how did Jesus react? He said and did nothing. He went quietly and in a dignified manner to his place without protest. He cared little for status games. He did not care how others ranked him, for he knew who he was and what God thought of him, and that was all that mattered. He was often to subvert their games of challenge and response and turn their notions of honor and shame upside down.

Feasts were never held in secret; this was an open society. Everybody knew everybody else's business, especially since no one was considered simply as an individual. Each person was embedded in a family, a tribe, a village, an area. Since feasts were part of the honor maintenance system, it was in the host's interest to display his guest list. This was a way of letting some people know they had not been invited.

So, this prostitute—quite well-known, of course, since theirs was a public profession in those days—would have heard Jesus was going to be at this feast. She also would have known something of the mentality of all those male guests, since she had probably serviced most of them at one time or another. She would have known how Jesus would be treated, and no doubt set out to get back at those pretentious men who claimed such high honor and moral rectitude.

Since the meal proper had started, there was no slave on duty at the entrance to do the washing of feet of guests. And since doors were kept open during the day so passers-by could see how lavishly the host had feted his guests, the prostitute had no difficulty entering the house. She went straight in and knew exactly where to find Jesus—at the bottom of the status line.

She stood behind the couch and reached over to where Jesus' feet were just over the edge. She did not face him, for that would have been to cause offense to him. (Remember in the house of Martha and Mary, how Mary sat at Jesus' feet, facing him, for she was a good woman and not a prostitute?) She then took off his sandals, bathed his dusty feet with her tears, wiped them with her hair and kissed them, and then anointed them with fragrant oil.

Notice her tears. They were out of place, and therefore a cause of ritual uncleanness. Her tears falling on Jesus caused him to be ritually unclean, thus making it dangerous for all the other guests who might now brush up against him. Should he now place his hand into a plate of food he would make it unclean and therefore inedible. In such an event the whole gathering would have erupted into a loud protest. Many guests would have immediately left had not Jesus started to talk to Simon, the host.

This prostitute knew exactly what she was doing. She knew how Jesus would have been treated by Simon, and she had decided to make her own protest on behalf of someone who had shown a deep understanding of the women who had no option other than turning to prostitution in order to survive in this male-dominated world. (We must remember that women without menfolk as their sponsors had no way of earning their own living except by prostitution. Jewish women did not easily turn to prostitution.)

She believed her action was in better taste than Simon's and would be a brave way of showing up the hypocrisy of all these men who were about to try and mock Jesus.

Luke gives us Simon's silent response to this outrage: "If he were a prophet, he would have known who and what sort of woman this is who is touching him."

This gives us an important clue about why Simon invited Jesus in the first place. He wanted to play games with Jesus and test out his ability to know the future and read people's minds. Now we can get a glimpse of the kind of games these guests were soon to play on Jesus.

There are some who believe Simon himself actually arranged for this woman to gate-crash his own feast, but I do not think it necessary to invent this idea. In Simon's mind, Jesus was living up to what he, Simon, thought of him in the first place—a dishonorable artisan who had no right to be telling others how to live honorably.

But Jesus was a prophet and read Simon's mind. But he didn't need to, actually. He knew what Simon had been up to when he invited him to a feast with those who deemed themselves Jesus' superiors. Jesus confronted Simon with a riddle about two debtors who owed different amounts to the same creditor.

We need to remember this was not like today, when you can decide to arrange a loan to pay for a car or a house. In those times peasants and peasant farmers were forced into debt to their landlords because of the rapacity of the landlords. Often small landowning farmers were forced to sell their farms and become tenant farmers, getting even further into debt in order to survive. Debt was not a voluntary arrangement, but the result of structural greed. And Simon knew this.

When Jesus asked which debtor would love his creditor more when both debts were canceled, Simon answered, "The one, I suppose, to whom he forgave more." Simon could not imagine any debtor loving his creditor, since it was the creditor who caused the debt in the first place.

It was, in fact, a trick question from Jesus. Love is not the response of someone forced into debt by a creditor's greed and rapacity. Simon knew the decision to cancel the debt made sound economic sense. It guaranteed the loyalty of the debtor, and, since the creditor owned the farm, it was better to cut his losses and let the debtor work harder to make sure there was no further need to get into debt again.

But Jesus had an important point to make, "Her sins, which are many, are forgiven, for she loved much; but he who is forgiven little, loves little."

Jesus turned his clever question around, making the point that love, not greed, can beget forgiveness. Because she showed Jesus such love and concern, her sins—her debts to a rather different kind of creditor, God—were forgiven. This is not the case where God as a harsh and greedy creditor forces people into debt and then out of some selfish concern for the divine reputation, cancels the debt. This is the elder brother welcoming a loving but rejected member of the community into the surrogate family of God and placing her on an equal footing with all the other members of his family by canceling her sins—her debts to God and the community. Her love for Jesus and her desire to serve him moved him to cancel her debts.

He then formally made public what had already happened between them, and said, "Your sins are forgiven. Your faith in me and in God has brought you wholeness; go in peace." Notice, he did not say to her, "Go, and sin no more," as he had to the woman taken in adultery. That woman had a choice about the way she lived: the prostitute did not. Jesus knew she had no option but to continue in her prostitution unless she could find a family to adopt her. The surrogate family of God had to wait until after Jesus' resurrection and ascension before the family members shared their goods and prevented widows and other single women from being enslaved in prostitution.

Simon's scheme to embarrass Jesus did not succeed. Instead, his own attitudes were shown up, and he was forced to learn the lesson that his wealth and position did not entitle him to play with the feelings and sensitivities of others. The prostitute learned that love and commitment from the heart bring their own reward, irrespective of her place in society.

I have gone into more detail here because we can learn much from this narrative. We can reflect on the way we play the status stakes and how we sometimes make fun of those we see as either above us or below us. We see the redemptive power of selfless love and commitment to others, and to God.

I wonder if any of us can match the love and commitment to Jesus shown by this wonderful prostitute.

The Women Who Acted as Patrons

> Soon afterward he went on through cities and villages, preaching and bringing the good news of the kingdom of God. And the twelve were with him, and also some women who had been healed of evil spirits and infirmities: Mary, called Magdalene, from whom seven demons had gone out, and Joanna, the wife of Chuza, Herod's steward, and Susanna, and many others, who provided for them out of their means.
>
> *(Lk. 8:1-3; Mat. 27:55-56; and Mk.15:40-41)*

Luke mentions that several women accompanied Jesus and the twelve on some of their missions throughout Galilee, and "ministered to them out of their means"—to render the Greek more accurately.

In Jewish society of that time this was a very rebellious thing for women to do. This was more than just cooking and serving meals. If a band of itinerant men needed someone to cook for them, they used a male slave. The idea of a group of women going around with these men and ministering to them was unheard of. Where did they sleep at night? Did they journey separately from the men? Why were they not at home looking after their own menfolk? Women who traveled for purposes other than shopping and visiting relatives were always regarded with suspicion.

Luke said that they were women "who had been healed of evil spirits and infirmities." This meant that their response to the healing Jesus brought into their lives was to provide for him and the twelve out of their own means. Thus, Jesus and his disciples did not need to beg food and accommodation as they journeyed.

Luke named three of these women: Mary from Magdala, out of whom Jesus had cast seven demons; Joanna wife of Chuza, Herod's steward; and Susanna.

In that society, as in the Greco-Roman world of the time, women were never named in their own right. You will look in vain for the names of women in honorary inscriptions without also finding them named as the wife of, or the daughter of, or the sister or mother of some male person. The only exceptions were widows of extremely famous and powerful people.

It is important, then, to realize that when in the gospels a woman is named without reference to a male sponsor, such a woman is a woman of shame. Mary of Magdala was shameful because of her demon possession; Susanna is unknown, but because she was either sick or demon-possessed she would have been regarded as shameful. Joanna's sponsor is named: Chuza, a powerful member of the royal household of King Herod. She was the only honorable woman named in that trio. But by leaving her husband and journeying with this band of men she brought dishonor to her husband. We are not told how he handled that, but my guess is he found life in Herod's court rather difficult!

That Jesus accepted the personal ministrations of women who were regarded as shameful says a great deal about his attitude regarding the customs of his days. But that they dared to be so public in their sponsorship of Jesus in the face of public outrage says something about their determination to respond to Jesus as women in their own right.

If a woman was seen as an object of shame, her husband or father or son was never named in association with her because this would extend the shame to him. Similarly, if a woman was named as being demon-possessed, her husband was never named.

It is also worth remembering that two of those women were chosen to be the first witnesses to the Risen Christ.

So we find a significant number of women who stepped right outside of their social position and demanded to serve Jesus in their own way. In each case Jesus not only approved of their actions, but praised them.

It is also interesting to note that most of these women served in ways men refused.

Called to Serve

The First Witnesses to the Resurrection of Jesus

But on the first day of the week, at early dawn, they went to the tomb, taking the spices which they had prepared. And they found the stone rolled away from the tomb, but when they went in they

did not find the body. While they were perplexed about this, behold, two men stood by them in dazzling apparel; and as they were
frightened and bowed their faces to the ground, the men said to
them, "Why do you seek the living among the dead? Remember
how he told you, while he was still in Galilee, that the Son of Man
must be delivered into the hands of sinful men, and be crucified,
and on the third day rise." And they remembered his words, and
returning from the tomb they told all this to the eleven and to all
the rest. Now it was Mary Magdalene and Joanna and Mary the
mother of James and the other women with them who told this to
the apostles; but these words seemed to them an idle tale, and
they did not believe them.

(Lk. 24:1-11 and Mat. 28:1-8; Mk. 16:1-8; Jn. 20:1-2)

In those days the word of a woman in a law court was never trusted.
Her testimony had to be validated by at least two suitable males. Bear
in mind that it is not too many years—in my lifetime—since the word
of a pregnant woman could not be used on its own in the law courts
of many Western countries.

The women who went to the tomb to complete the task of embalming the body of Jesus were a motley lot—Magdalene, the mother of
James, Salome, Joanna and a few others who had attended Jesus from
the beginning of the movement in Galilee, and who had done what the
male disciples refused to do: keep Jesus company during his crucifixion. An interesting and disparate group: one had co-habited with seven
demons, two were wives of fishing entrepreneurs and honored in their
village, one was the wife of a top official in Herod's household, and
others that had sufficient money to hire servants to do their household
chores while they wandered around with Jesus and the twelve.

The other interesting thing about this group is that none of them
is related by blood to Jesus. The task of embalming was normally the
responsibility of the blood relatives of the deceased. Where were Jesus'
mother and his sisters? It seems the women who went to the tomb regarded themselves as members of the surrogate family Jesus had talked
about—the family that had God as father and himself as elder brother,
with all others as his siblings.

For all their money and dedication to the Messiah, they did not qualify in the eyes of the men who ran their society to be official witnesses to the most important phenomenon in human history—the resurrection of Jesus. Yet God chose them to be the first bearers of this momentous event, making God the most outrageous God in human history.

You would have thought God knew better than that. You would have thought God would have chosen to use the most respectable, trustworthy, honorable and socially acceptable people—men—to be the official heralds of the message that "He is risen!"

But no! Our outrageous God chose women, and these women were rebellious enough to accept this task without question and expect they would be believed when they told the men this most unlikely of all truths: "Jesus is alive and will meet them in Galilee."

In John's gospel, of course, they are not believed until Peter and John check out the grave for themselves, thus fulfilling the requirement of two males validating the women's testimony. Luke says of the men: "these words seemed to them an idle tale, and they did not believe them."

When Paul gives the list of those people to whom Jesus first revealed himself, you will notice a significant omission.

> For I delivered to you as of first importance what I also received, that Christ died for our sins in accordance with the scriptures, that he was buried, that he was raised on the third day in accordance with the scriptures, and that he appeared to Cephas, then to the twelve. Then he appeared to more than five hundred brethren at one time, most of whom are still alive, though some have fallen asleep. Then he appeared to James, then to all the apostles. Last of all, as to one untimely born, he appeared also to me.
>
> *(I Cor. 15:3-8)*

All the gospels indicate women were the first people to see Jesus alive and hear his voice. Yet here is Paul reporting what he had been told by Peter and James, that they had been the first.

I wonder how Mary and her companions would have felt had they been handed a copy of Paul's letter to the Corinthians?

Outrageous women will usually be put down by men, especially in the church.

When God called upon women to serve with Jesus, God was taking a risk that the work of Jesus would be disregarded and dishonored in a society that placed little value on the word and work of women outside the household. Yet these same women were staunch and loyal followers of Jesus, standing beside him at the crucifixion when all but one of the men had run off in fear. Without the selfless devotion and commitment of these women, the actual work of Jesus and the twelve would have been much more difficult. They made it possible for the men to give all their time to the proclamation of the kingdom without having to take time and energy to organize food and accommodation.

Specially Chosen

This next group of women were specially chosen to make unique contributions to the work of God in the world—work that was almost indispensable. When seen from the perspective of the first century of our era, these women were being called upon to take a place well outside the one prescribed for them by men.

Elizabeth

After these days his wife Elizabeth conceived, and for five months she hid herself, saying, "Thus the Lord has done to me in the days when he looked on me, to take away my reproach among men."

In those days Mary arose and went with haste into the hill country, to a city of Judah, and she entered the house of Zechariah and greeted Elizabeth. And when Elizabeth heard the greeting of Mary, the babe leaped in her womb; and Elizabeth was filled with the Holy Spirit and she exclaimed with a loud cry, "Blessed are you among women, and blessed is the fruit of your womb! And why is this granted me, that the mother of my Lord should come to me? For behold, when the voice of your greeting came to my ears, the babe in my womb leaped for joy. And blessed is she who believed that there would be a fulfillment of what was spoken to her from the Lord."

And on the eighth day they came to circumcise the child; and they would have named him Zechariah after his father, but his mother said, "Not so; he shall be called John." And they said to her, "None of your kindred is called by this name." And they made signs to his father, inquiring what he would have him called. And he asked for a writing tablet, and wrote, "His name is John." And they all marveled.

(Lk. 1:24-25, 39-45, 59-63)

We first meet Elizabeth, mother-to-be of John the Baptizer, in Luke 1:5-7. She is described as the wife of Zechariah, who was a priest of the division of Abijah. She herself was from a priestly family, it being quite common for Jewish priests to seek out suitable wives from priestly families. She and her husband were "righteous before God, walking in all the commandments and ordinances of the Lord blameless."

But she was barren and past the period of her fertility.

We again need to remember a woman's primary role was to give birth to children for her husband. This was an important part of her maintaining the honor of her husband's name in the family and village. Heirless husbands were objects of shame and reproach, while barren wives had no hope of ever being accepted in the community. The story of the treatment of Hannah in I Samuel 1:5-8 was typical.

Until a wife bore her husband a son, her position as a blood relative in the family was never secure.

The second-century *Infancy Gospel of James* provided an interesting insight into just how strong this bias was. Joachim, the father of the Virgin Mary, had the right to be the first to offer his gifts to the Lord, but was prevented from doing so because he had no children. After searching the records he found he was the only one in his tribe over several generations to be childless. He was so ashamed he went out into the wilderness and fasted.[2]

Elizabeth, then, was a source of her husband's loss of honor in his community, even though he performed in an honorable profession — the priesthood. The pressure laid upon Zechariah to take a young wife and raise up at least one son would have been enormous. However, he remained true to his commitment to Elizabeth, praying constantly for a solution to the problem of his loss of honor.

Since it was the man who suffered the dishonor, it was to the man that God sent the angel Gabriel with the assurance God would resolve Zechariah's problem. His wife would conceive in her old age and have a son, who would take up a most important role: that of being the new Elijah to prepare Israel for the coming of the Messiah.

When she became aware of being pregnant in fulfillment of the angel's words, Elizabeth hid herself from public gaze by staying indoors for two reasons: to make sure no one could accuse her of sexual misdemeanor by having intercourse with a young man, and to wait until she was obviously pregnant so no one could accuse her of lying.

During the sixth month of her pregnancy she was visited by a relative, Mary, the mother-to-be of Jesus. No sooner were the customary greetings over than Elizabeth's fetus made an uncharacteristic movement inside her. The conversation between Elizabeth and Mary was typical women's talk of the day, always done behind closed doors. The fact Luke was given access to some of the details meant he may have had a special relationship with Mary, for none of this was reported in the other gospels.

Elizabeth's response to Mary's news was one of joy for her kinswoman. She did not bemoan her own life of barrenness up to this time, but shared in Mary's delight at having her first child at such a young age. She also felt a special privilege at being the only one to be told of Mary's coming pregnancy.

Her great shout of praise, "Blessed are you among women, and blessed is the fruit of your womb!" has become enshrined in Christian liturgy and prayer down the ages.

We need to be constantly reminded that women's beliefs and outbursts of praise and prophecy were not valued in the society. That they have persisted in the tradition and scriptures is to be seen as unusual and at risk of being decried by men.

In due time Elizabeth gave birth to her son and announced his name was John, not Zechariah or whatever Zechariah's father's name was. Such naming caused consternation in the whole community, since the names of male children were important matters of the way families were bonded together. The father was required to assent to the name as a guarantee that he accepted the child as his own. The giving of a name not included in the family networks was highly suspicious, and could lead to the suggestion that perhaps Zechariah was not the father.

But Zechariah, still dumb from the action of Gabriel because of Zechariah's doubts, was called upon to name his son. He did so in writing and confirmed the name John. Immediately he regained his speech and praised God.

The reaction of the whole community was predictable. The whole of the hill country in which Zechariah lived buzzed for weeks. That a woman well past her fertile period should give birth was awesome enough—reminiscent of Abraham's wife, Sarah. But the name given to the baby, John—"God has been gracious"—meant that in some way he would not be embedded in the family. And that proved to be the case when John left home to take up his residence in the wilderness—not to follow his father's profession of priest, but to be the second Elijah and announce the coming of the Messiah and the need of all people to prepare themselves for this coming.

Elizabeth faded from view from here onward. She was now, at long last and in her old age, fully accepted as a wife and mother. All those years of shame and heartbreak ended. Her husband was restored to his honorable position as head of a household that had a son.

Her faithfulness in the midst of such community pressures was something we take too little account of. It was no wonder God chose her—for she certainly proved God right!

Mary the Mother of Jesus

So little was known of this Mary that a family had to be invented for her in the second century. Thus, the *Infancy Gospel of James* reported her mother was Anna of Bethlehem and her father Joachim of Nazareth. We know of one sister from John 19:25, where her sister was among the women who stood by the cross of Jesus.

It would seem she was from the house and lineage of David, sharing that tribal identity with her betrothed, Joseph.

It is something worth pondering on that God should choose for the mother of the Messiah a young woman whose father is not named and whose family tree is not outlined. It is even more amazing to remember that Matthew and Luke both proudly list the lineage of David, right back to Adam, when it was not to be Joseph's sperm that would help in the procreation process!

What we have here is the usual emphasis on the male head of the house with whom all the household is identified. His genealogy provided not only the identity, but the honor into which his wife, children and household slaves were embedded. Provided the wife did not come from a foreign family or was not a slave, her genealogy was not as critical.

> In the sixth month the angel Gabriel was sent from God to a city of Galilee named Nazareth, to a virgin betrothed to a man whose name was Joseph, of the house of David; and the virgin's name was Mary. And he came to her and said, "Hail, O favored one, the Lord is with you!" But she was greatly troubled at the saying, and considered in her mind what sort of greeting this might be. And the angel said to her, "Do not be afraid, Mary, for you have found favor with God. And behold, you will conceive in your womb and bear a son, and you shall call his name Jesus.
>
> "He will be great, and will be called the Son of the Most High; and the Lord God will give to him the throne of his father David, and he will reign over the house of Jacob for ever; and of his kingdom there will be no end."
>
> And Mary said to the angel, "How shall this be, since I have no husband?" And the angel said to her,
>
> "The Holy Spirit will come upon you,
> and the power of the Most High will overshadow you;
> therefore the child to be born will be called holy,
> the Son of God.
>
> "And behold, your kinswoman Elizabeth in her old age has also conceived a son; and this is the sixth month with her who was called barren. For with God nothing will be impossible." And Mary said, "Behold, I am the handmaid of the Lord; let it be to me according to your word." And the angel departed from her.
>
> *(Lk. 1:26-38)*

Here God's angel goes directly to the woman, not to her husband or betrothed as in the case of Elizabeth. This is in itself unusual. Once

Mary had been betrothed to Joseph, she was embedded in him and his family, with him as her sponsor.

Betrothal was much more public than in the West today. The match between the groom and bride was formally conducted in a public ceremony in the village square. Both family heads would have been involved in lengthy negotiations regarding the dowry and the living arrangements for the bride. The contract was usually arranged by the two fathers, with the mothers having significant input. The contract was announced and signed on a well advertised day in the midst of the villagers.

The only delay for the couple was the time it would take to arrange the wedding ceremony. The important point was they were in fact married by the exchange of contracts at the betrothal ceremony, but did not live together until the actual wedding ceremony. Until then, the bride-to-be was not available for social gatherings and had to behave as though she was already a wife. Should any man have intercourse with her, that would be an act of adultery and they could both be stoned. If the husband-to-be wanted to pull out of the betrothal, he had to get a bill of divorce.

Thus, when Gabriel came to Mary, she was already "married" to Joseph. All communication should have been addressed to him and not to her. This was one reason, no doubt, why Matthew, who was much more careful to show that his central characters kept the social niceties, omitted the visit of Gabriel to Mary, but has the angel visit Joseph to assure him Mary's pregnancy was not the result of an adulterous act, but caused by the direct intervention of God's Holy Spirit.

Thus, Mary had two good reasons to be troubled by Gabriel's visit. The first was that he came to her and not to Joseph. How on earth would she ever be able to tell Joseph about this? There were no male witnesses to this visitation. The second reason was the greeting given her by Gabriel: "Rejoice! O one on whom God has been pleased to endow grace! The Lord be with you!"

Mary, being a modest and humble woman, was deeply troubled by this greeting. Why was not her betrothed husband thus greeted? She had no status or honor apart from him. Gabriel reassured her and gave her the prophecy that her son was to be the Messiah and ruler over the future house of David. But how can this possibly be? She had not been publicly married and therefore could not have had intercourse with Joseph. Indeed, she was not allowed to mix with any male company until the village wedding.

Gabriel explained what was to happen to her. God's Holy Spirit would cause her to become pregnant in a way that ensured the child would be male and would be "holy": that is, dedicated to the service of God. It is important to remember here that "holiness" describes the space and purpose, not the inner quality. The baby, Jesus, was to be dedicated to serve God—indeed would be, by act of God, the Son of God.

What Mary was being told is that God will assume the traditional role of husband in her case: God would make her a mother and would protect her.

It is as though Mary was being given the news that God was going to set up a surrogate family to replace the family of Israel; God would be the father, she the mother and Jesus the elder brother. All subsequent children she bore to Joseph would be junior to Jesus.

This notion of the surrogate family was to be the model early Christianity used to explain its movement.

Mary's response was simple but honest. She couldn't really comprehend what it all meant, but said to Gabriel, "Behold I am the slave of God; let it be to me according to your word."

She called herself a female slave, the one that waits on her master and does his every bidding without question, without pay and without any redress. A slave has no rights to family and kinship, no rights to personal possessions and no will. Hers is an unquestioning and absolute response of submission to the God who sent Gabriel with this message.

She was reassured by the knowledge given her by Gabriel that her relative Elizabeth was already six months pregnant, in spite of her age. As with Elizabeth, Mary's son was named ahead of time by God. This would have been perceived to confer a great deal of honor on the boy when born. In both cases, the name is not from the genealogy, thus signifying a special holiness for each boy.

After recovering from what must have been a rather traumatic experience for her, Mary went off to see her cousin Elizabeth. Notice, she did not go and see Joseph. They are not supposed to mix socially without others present until the wedding day. And who would believe this fantastic story of the visitation by Gabriel and the message she had been given? Certainly none of her friends and family would ever believe God chose to speak to her and not first to Joseph.

I have already dealt with the meeting between Mary and Elizabeth, so I want to concentrate on the prophecy Mary uttered.

> And Mary said,
>> "My soul magnifies the Lord,
>> and my spirit rejoices in God my Savior,
>> for he has regarded the low estate of his handmaiden.
>> For behold, henceforth all generations will call me blessed;
>> for he who is mighty has done great things for me,
>> and holy is his name.
>> And his mercy is on those who fear him
>> from generation to generation.
>> He has shown strength with his arm,
>> he has scattered the proud in the imagination of their hearts,
>> he has put down the mighty from their thrones,
>> and exalted those of low degree;
>> he has filled the hungry with good things,
>> and the rich he has sent away empty.
>> He has helped his servant Israel,
>> in remembrance of his mercy,
>> as he spoke to our fathers,
>> to Abraham and to his posterity for ever."
> And Mary remained with her about three months, and returned to her home.
>
> *(Lk. 1:46-56)*

Let me offer the following translation in order to counter our overfamiliarity with the words we use so often in our liturgies. I am trying to let this Mediterranean young woman speak to us in her own words.

> With my mind I exalt the Lord,
> and with my whole inner being I exult in God my redeemer,
> because God has taken note of my slavelike subservience.
> You will see that from now on all generations will declare

    that God has treated me as special,
    because the Powerful One has done mighty things for me.
    Holy be God's Name,
    and divine mercy continue from generation after generation
    to the ones making obeisance to the Powerful One.
    With an arm the Lord creates sovereignty
    and banishes the arrogant in the conceit of their hearts.
    The Powerful One has dethroned authorities
    but has promoted subservients;
    the starving ones God has satiated with good
    and the self-satisfied dismissed empty.
    God has been fully devoted to Israel the beloved one
    as a memorial to divine mercy;
    just as was said to our ancestors,
    to Abraham and to his descendants for ever.

No translation from one language to another can fully reflect all that is going on in the text and in the speaker. But I hope this translation may cause you to think again about these words.

Mary was honored by the angel Gabriel in a way she could not believe she deserved, poured out her heart, not only in heartfelt thanks to God for choosing her for such an honored position as the mother of the Messiah, but in a burst of pent-up hope for the revolution her selection may bring about.

Male oral poetry was usually a rather formal, public affair—the putting together of familiar sayings from the Psalms and the prophets. You have only to read the outburst of Zechariah in the temple at the circumcision of his son to see that. It is full of the usual hopes and prayers that occur in each act of worship and prayer.

But women's oral poetry, which was usually said in private when women got together for their socializing and bonding, was much more likely to be revolutionary—going into subjects women were not supposed to even think about, let alone sing about.

Mary's song—and she would have sung it to a familiar chant—is full of topics women would never discuss in front of their menfolk. She characterized the God of Israel as one who has directly chosen a woman to take part in the founding of the new Israel. She has suggested that the God of Israel has mercy on all people, not just on Israel. She has described God as overturning the economic and social structures of Jewish society. She has claimed that all this revolutionary activity by God was in fact all there in the promises made to Abraham, Isaac and Jacob.

Had Mary sung that song before her betrothed Joseph and in her village square, she would have been stoned for blasphemy!

Luke says Mary stayed with Elizabeth for about three months before returning home. That means she left a day or two before the birth of John, helping her cousin Elizabeth during those last difficult weeks of pregnancy when she would need the kind of support that only a woman could give. Remember, Elizabeth had hidden herself when she fell pregnant, so she would not have had anyone to call on.

Luke does not tell us exactly when Mary conceived, but it could well have been soon after Gabriel's visit, so that her pregnancy would have become evident while she was there. We can see in these two women a great strength of purpose, and in Mary a particular sense of destiny for herself and the son in her womb. But this sense of destiny would be sorely tried and she stumbled from time to time. After the birth of Jesus and the visitation of the shepherds, Luke writes "she kept all these things, pondering them in her heart."

Luke gives us clues as to the social status of Joseph. The baby was dressed in swaddling clothes, usually thought of as the clothing of the poor. The practice of wrapping babies tightly to restrict their freedom was a common one at the time, and still persists in some cultures. Joseph was an artisan and would not have had the resources to clothe his son in expensive garments. It was only after the visit of the Magi, with their expensive gifts, that there was any spare money available.

This Mediterranean virgin, who was burdened with a secret she could share only with her cousin Elizabeth, faced a difficult time ahead, with suspicions of adultery against her and claims of illegitimacy against her son.

We see her next quietly presenting her son for circumcision and hearing the prophecies of Simeon and Anna. Every year at Passover, she and Joseph took him to the temple at Jerusalem. And then, when Jesus was twelve, they made the special journey so he could undergo the ritual of becoming a "son of the law." This marked his progress into puberty and the right to take some part in synagogue worship. It also marked his transition from the world of his mother to the world of his father. From this moment on, Joseph took over as leading parent, with Mary now in the background.

The emotional attachment of the son to his mother will never disappear, and it will often be harder for the mother to give up the education and discipline of her son to her husband. But this is the way of the Mediterranean family, and both Jesus and Mary must conform.

> Now his parents went to Jerusalem every year at the feast of the Passover. And when he was twelve years old, they went up according to custom; and when the feast was ended, as they were returning, the boy Jesus stayed behind in Jerusalem. His parents did not know it, but supposing him to be in the company they went a day's journey, and they sought him among their kinsfolk and acquaintances; and when they did not find him, they returned to Jerusalem, seeking him. After three days they found him in the temple, sitting among the teachers, listening to them and asking them questions; and all who heard him were amazed at his understanding and his answers. And when they saw him they were astonished; and his mother said to him, "Son, why have you treated us so? Behold, your father and I have been looking for you anxiously." And he said to them, "How is it that you sought me? Did you not know that I must be in my Father's house?" And they did not understand the saying which he spoke to them. And he went down with them and came to Nazareth, and was obedient to them; and his mother kept all these things in her heart.
>
> *(Lk. 2:41-51)*

What is noticeable in this story is that, while Jesus made the transition from the female world to the male world quite readily, Mary had not. When Jesus was missing and his parents returned to Jerusalem to find him still in the temple, it is Mary and not Joseph who had the first word. "Son, why have you treated us so? Behold, your father and I have been looking for you anxiously." Mary should have left Joseph to handle this situation.

Jesus respectfully rebuked her for not knowing where he would be, showing a self awareness about his new status as the son of his Father.

Once again Luke says Mary kept all these things in her heart.

From here on, Mary surfaced rarely in the gospel narrative. Her son took up the trade of his father, as was expected. Once Joseph died, Jesus took over as head of the household. We know of two brothers and several sisters Jesus would have been expected to care for. He was now the sponsor of his mother and sisters. Family honor demanded he provide for them, and for his sisters he had to find suitable husbands and dowries. He would help his younger brothers set up their own households as they came of marriageable age.

When Jesus, aged thirty, walked out of that house to begin his messianic mission, he was perceived by his village and family to have acted dishonorably. Leaving his mother and sisters without a suitable sponsor was unpardonable, and at times he would be reminded of that. I mention this here in a book about women because it is an important factor in understanding the behavior of Mary.

Mark shows Mary trying to get Jesus back into the house. He had been doing a great deal of healing and casting out of demons.

> Then he went home; and the crowd came together again, so that they could not even eat. And when his family heard it, they went out to seize him, for people were saying, "he is beside himself." And the scribes who came down from Jerusalem said, "He is possessed by Beelzebub, and by the prince of demons he casts out demons"... And his mother and his brothers came; and standing outside they sent to him and called him.
>
> *(Mk. 3:19-22, 31; Mat. 12:46-50; and Lk. 8:19-21)*

Mary was still dealing with the dishonor Jesus had brought to her husband's name, and now he was accused of being insane—even possessed by the very demons he was casting out of other people. She wanted to get him inside the house and out of the public view.

The only other time Mary comes into the narrative in her own right, apart from the crucifixion scene and being with the eleven after

Jesus' resurrection, is at the wedding feast where Jesus turned the water into wine.

> On the third day there was a marriage at Cana in Galilee, and the mother of Jesus was there; Jesus also was invited to the marriage, with his disciples. When the wine failed, the mother of Jesus said to him, "They have no wine." And Jesus said to her, "O woman, what have you to do with me? My hour has not yet come." His mother said to the servants, "Do whatever he tells you." Now six stone jars were standing there, for the Jewish rites of purification, each holding twenty or thirty gallons. Jesus said to them, "Fill the jars with water." And they filled them up to the brim. He said to them, "Now draw some out, and take it to the steward of the feast." So they took it. When the steward of the feast tasted the water now become wine, and did not know where it came from (though the servants who had drawn the water knew), the steward of the feast called the bridegroom and said to him, "Every man serves the good wine first; and when men have drunk freely, then the poor wine; but you have kept the good wine until now."
>
> *(Jn. 2:1-10)*

A marriage is a village affair where two families are bonded in public. The two families, not the groom and bride, are the chief focus. There have been months of negotiation, the public exchange of contracts and then the feast at which the two meet for the first time since the betrothal.

The fact that Mary was there with Jesus and the twelve disciples showed they were close friends of the two families. This was made even more obvious when you realize Mary was involved with the catering. The main feast was usually in the bride's parents' home, and was the main preliminary to the groom conducting the bride to his home for the consummation. But in this case it seems to have been held in the groom's parents' house. This meant Mary was probably a close relative of the groom's family.

A crisis loomed as the wine supply dwindles to a dangerously low point. The honor of the groom's father was threatened. He had asserted the true status of his family and possessions when bargaining with the bride's family about the size of the dowry he expected from them. He did his best to provide a son that would keep his honorable position in the community intact.

If the wine runs out, the whole community—not just those attending the feast—would accuse him of acting above his status, pretending he had more money than he really had. Going off to the nearest wine seller and trying to negotiate more wine would have added to that, for the vintner would seize the opportunity to double his prices!

Mary went to her son with a plea that he do something to save the situation. The honor of her friend's husband had to be saved.

Since her own husband was dead, Mary's status was embedded in her son's. Although he had dishonored the family by leaving home and walking away from his responsibilities, she saw an opportunity for Jesus to rehabilitate the family name. If she could persuade him to save the day in some attention-getting way, the community may give her back her husband's honor.

But Jesus, as always, was not about to become involved in the honor-shame games of his community. His enigmatic reply, as the Greek has it, "O woman, what (is it) to me and to you? My hour is not yet" is telling Mary that what she wants he cannot give in the way she longs for. She wanted some public affirmation of her son's power and position; he solved the problem without drawing attention to himself at all.

Jesus' moment of supreme honor is death on the shameful and dishonoring cross. He would do nothing to maintain his social honor as perceived by his community. The miracle he performed was seen only by the slaves who served the guests with the wine. The comment of the chairman of the feast that this lot of wine was of superior quality was a further sadness for Mary. If only the whole gathering could have known it was her dishonorable son who had saved the occasion from disaster by changing water into this wonderful wine!

Mary needed to be seen as she really was—a true Mediterranean woman, embedded first in her husband and then in her son, finally handed on to the apostle John to be embedded in his family until her death.

In many ways she acted outrageously in her early years; but, once Jesus began his mission, she was to be sorely tested as her expectations of honor for her son and herself gradually faded. Sadly, we hear nothing from her after Jesus' resurrection, so we have no way of knowing how she reacted to the kingdom as it actually emerged. In true Mediterranean style, the men of the early church drew no attention to her whatsoever.

The Adulteress

Including the woman taken into adultery in the list of those especially chosen seems strange at first glance. But, whereas the first two women were chosen by God to play important roles in the kingdom, this woman was chosen by Jesus' enemies to play what they expected would be a crucial role in dishonoring him. In the event, Jesus turned the tables on them and used her to make an important statement about the status of women in society.

> The scribes and the Pharisees brought a woman who had been caught in adultery, and placing her in the midst they said to him, "Teacher, this woman has been caught in the act of adultery. Now in the law Moses commanded us to stone such. What do you say about her?" This they said to test him, that they might have some charge to bring against him. Jesus bent down and wrote with his finger on the ground. And as they continued to ask him, he stood up and said to them, "Let him who is without sin among you be the first to throw a stone at her." And once more he bent down and wrote with his finger on the ground. But when they heard it, they went away, one by one, beginning with the eldest, and Jesus was left alone with the woman standing before him. Jesus looked up and said to her, "Woman, where are they? Has no one condemned you?" She said, "No one, Lord." And Jesus said, "Neither do I condemn you; go, and do not sin again."
>
> *(Jn. 8:3-11)*

Adultery was a sin against the husband. The wife was embedded in her husband, and had no place at all outside of his status. His honor was maintained by her sexual faithfulness to him, while any unfaithfulness brought him shame. Wives were expected to be virgins on marriage; any signs of a lack of virginity annulled the marriage. Any evidence of her sexual misconduct as a wife meant instant divorce. The husband had no choice in the matter. This was an open society—nothing happened behind closed doors that did not come out into the open fairly quickly. Privacy as a value was unknown.

This woman must have been married for a charge of adultery to be leveled, for a married man having sexual intercourse with a single woman was not adultery. She was chosen by Jesus' enemies to trick him into denying the validity of the Mosaic Law. No doubt his liberal attitude toward women had become well known, and they wanted to use this as a way of attacking him. If he said she should not be stoned to death for her crime, he could be brought before the temple authorities and charged with teaching others to break the law. If he agreed to her stoning, they would be able to take him before the Roman authorities and charge him with breaking their law, since it was illegal for Jews in Israel to carry out a death sentence without first getting the approval of the Roman governor.

Of course, their plot did not work because Jesus turned the tables on them by challenging their own law-keeping standards. "Let the one who has never broken a law throw the first stone." These men knew each other pretty well, and knew that not one of them had ever been a perfect law keeper. For any man there to have picked up a stone would have been to make a claim to honor that all the others knew to be false. He would have been jeered at.

They all realized they have been outmaneuvered and gradually dispersed, beginning with the oldest and most respected, for these had the most to lose: only the young and foolish might try to tough it out.

The woman is left alone with Jesus. She has made no protest. She has not asked, "Why did you not bring the man too? It takes two to commit adultery." She could have claimed she was set up by one of those present, for how else could she have been seen in the act. Her adulterous partner could well have been among the accusers.

Jesus asked her a rather obvious question, "Has none of these man laid a formal charge against you?"

Her simply reply of "No one, sir" elicits Jesus' now famous words, "Neither do I lay any charge against you. Off you go and do not repeat the offense."

What is remarkable here is that Jesus did not question her to find out the truth. He accepted that she did commit the offense. But what is also remarkable is that, while Jesus did not condone this act of adultery, he did appear to suggest that divorce would not necessarily follow.

When asked about divorce in Mark's gospel, Jesus extended the meaning of divorce to a husband's unfaithfulness to his wife, thus giving married women the right to initiate divorce, a rare phenomenon in those days in Israel.[3]

This woman had been chosen by Jesus' enemies to be used against Jesus, but in the end was used against them. Her meekness and acceptance of the shameful situation she found herself in, and her reluctance to try extracting herself from what was clearly an injustice, resulted in her being forgiven. Can there be any fear that she would ever commit adultery again?

These three women were chosen as examples of the fact that God does not confine his prophetic word and demand of responsibility to men. Without the willing cooperation of women like these, even when it meant going against the customs and even the law of their day, the world and the church would be in a much poorer state.

Self-Servers

There are always those who care only about themselves and nothing about anyone else. This is not confined to men. Indeed, the Old Testament is replete with women who behaved badly.

The following two women, a mother and her daughter, are the only "bad" women named in the gospels. They belong to the family of Herod, and had an unsavory reputation.

Herodias and Her Daughter

For Herod had sent and seized John, and bound him in prison for the sake of Herodias, his brother Philip's wife; because he had married her. For John said to Herod, "It is not lawful for you to have your brother's wife." And Herodias had a grudge against him, and wanted to kill him. But she could not, for Herod feared John, knowing that he was a righteous and holy man, and kept him safe. When he heard him, he was much perplexed; and yet he heard him gladly. But an opportunity came when Herod on his birthday gave a banquet for his courtiers and officers and the leading men of Galilee. For when Herodias' daughter came in and danced, she pleased Herod and his guests; and the king said to the girl, "Ask me for whatever you wish, and I will grant it." And he vowed to her, "Whatever you ask me, I will give you, even half of my kingdom." And she went out, and said to her mother, "What shall I ask?" And she said, "The head of John the Baptist." And she came in immediately with haste to the king, and asked, saying, "I want you to give me at once the head of John the Baptist on a platter." And the king was exceedingly sorry; but because of his oaths and his guests he did not want to break his word to her. And immediately the king sent a soldier of the guard and gave orders to bring his head. He went and beheaded him in the prison, and brought his head on a platter, and gave it to the girl; and the girl gave it to her mother. When his disciples heard of it, they came and took his body, and laid it in a tomb.

(Mk. 6:16-29 and Mat. 14:1-12)

We know from Josephus[4], the Jewish historian of the first century of our era, that Herodias' daughter by her first husband, Philip, was called Salome.

Herod Antipas had been appointed tetrarch of Galilee in 4 B.C. Not content with the limited power he, a son of Herod the Great, had been given, he demanded to be a client king of Caesar. For such temerity, he was deposed and banished in A.D. 39. But while in power he seemed to arrogate to himself the title of king, which is why Mark called him king.

Herodias was herself a granddaughter of Herod the Great and also half-niece of Herod Antipas. She married Philip, a son of Herod the Great, and Philip the tetrarch of the gospel story. It was her daughter Salome who was married to Philip, her uncle. The whole Herodian family was riddled with incestuous relationships, so it is little wonder their history gets a little confused.

It seems John the Baptist publicly condemned Herod Antipas for divorcing his first wife, a Nabatean princess, in order to marry Herodias, also divorced from Herod Philip. Such public revelations of the powerful elite would certainly have been strongly disapproved of, and the Baptist was imprisoned, probably at the behest of Herodias, who stood to lose the most by his public revelations.

That Herod was afraid of John is an important marker of the respect and honor in which he was held by the people. It was this kind of fear and jealousy that was the eventual cause of Antipas' downfall. The public feast Herod organized to mark his own birthday was a typical act of honor maintenance. He did this because it was expected of him, not just because he was a generous and open-hearted ruler. Mark tells us who was invited: his court attendants, his army officers and the civic leaders of Galilee. So this was an important collection of the elite of Galilee.

When Salome came in to dance, she did a shameful thing. Dancing by women was only done before family and kin. That honorable men at the top of the ruling elite allowed such a shameful thing to happen meant their own loss of honor in the eyes of the rest of the community. This was further compounded by Herod allowing himself to become bewitched by the sensuousness of Salome's dancing. It became quite clear that all this was organized by the two women in order to extract something from Herod. Under normal circumstances he would never have allowed this to happen. When Herod in his besotted state offered her all she was entitled to receive as a woman, half his assets, she went straight to her mother. But this plot was not about money. It turned out to be a scheme to secure the execution of the hated Baptist.

By having Herod make his pledge before all these honored guests, the women made certain they had him trapped. There was no way he could crawl out from under. Had this happened at a private, family party, they would not have succeeded. Herod had to keep his pledge, no doubt glad in one way at not losing half of his assets to a woman he could never have for his own while his wife—her mother—was still alive.

We can only gaze in disgust and dismay at the sight of the bleeding head of John the Baptist, the last of the Hebrew prophets, sitting on a silver salver and being carried off in triumph by these two horrible women. Here were two women who knew how to manipulate the games of honor and shame among men to serve their own evil desires.

Women in Jesus' Parables

In the three parables that follow, Jesus used women to give a positive lesson on behavior that went outside the values women were to exemplify—purity and virginity. Proverbs 31:10-31 is typical of the "ideal woman" in the Mediterranean world. Her world was inside the home, industrious and managerial, allowing her husband to spend his time drinking coffee with the other husbands in the village square.

But Jesus shows women had far more to offer, even when some did not live up to their responsibilities.

The Ten Maidens

"Then the kingdom of heaven shall be compared to ten maidens who took their lamps and went to meet the bridegroom. Five of them were foolish, and five were wise. For when the foolish took their lamps, they took no oil with them; but the wise took flasks of oil with their lamps. As the bridegroom was delayed, they all slumbered and slept. But at midnight there was a cry, 'Behold, the bridegroom! Come out to meet him.' Then all those maidens rose and trimmed their lamps. And the foolish said to the wise, 'Give us some of your oil, for our lamps are going out.' But the wise replied, 'Perhaps there will not be enough for us and for you; go rather to the dealers and buy for yourselves.' And while they went to buy, the bridegroom came, and those who were ready went in with him to the marriage feast; and the door was shut. Afterward the other maidens came also, saying, 'Lord, lord, open to us.' But he replied, 'Truly, I say to you, I do not know you.' Watch therefore, for you know neither the day nor the hour.

(Mat. 25:1-13)

A wedding was a great social occasion for the whole village. The two families being united were extremely careful about making sure everything in the ceremonies and feasts reflected their social position.

This is a ten-bridesmaid wedding. It was a very important occasion for the super elite of the village. While everyone was able to come out and watch the activities, only the elites had been invited to the feast and formal occasions.

The particular part of the ceremony Jesus used for his parable was that moment when the groom left his parents' house to go to the bride's parents' place to conduct her to the house that would be his and his bride's. This house was usually within a stone's throw of his parents' house.

You will notice the Jews at some stage changed from the Genesis tradition (where the groom went to live with his bride's family) to the tradition here where the bride is re-embedded in her husband's family.

The groom left for his bride's parents' house and at this point the ten bridesmaids joined the procession to the groom's house. Here, all the official guests were already reclining and feasting, waiting for the couple to join them. At the end of the feast the groom would conduct his bride to the bedroom and consummate the marriage. He would then return to the feasters and display the bloodstained sheet that attested to his own masculinity and to his bride's virginity. This would be greeted with cheers and acclamations.

The honor of both sets of parents was very much at stake here. (It is interesting to note that this custom still prevails in many Mediterranean communities.)

In the parable, the groom delayed at his parents' house. Mothers the world over are always loath to give up their sons; while fathers want to make sure all the financial arrangements are in order. Whatever the reasons, the groom arrived late at his bride's house. All the ten bridesmaids had fallen asleep, the excitement of the occasion taking its toll. Their lamps had been lit to light up the entrance to the bride's parents house, but five of the lamps had gone out and there was no more oil to relight them. The five girls tried to persuade the others to share the remaining oil with them. But to no effect, for if the groom delayed too long, all the lamps would go out, and then where would the procession be!

It was off to the nearest oil supplier to wake him up in the dead of night and scrounge some oil from him. The fact that such merchants were at home and not at the wedding indicated how high up on the social scale were the people involved in this particular wedding. By the time they returned, the groom had arrived and taken his bride to his house.

The effect of their carelessness was to reduce the wedding from a ten-bridesmaid ceremony to a five-bridesmaid one, thus bringing dishonor to the groom's family, by whom they had been chosen. Not only had all these young virgins been carefully selected to make sure they belonged to the blood lines of both families, but their mothers would have spent days training them in the dances and songs they had to perform, and in making sure they knew how to dress and how to look after their lamps.

Their lack of attention to one detail—the amount of oil to take in order to account for any unusual delay on the part of the groom—led to spoiling the whole occasion.

In the parable Jesus calls them by a very terrible word. "Foolish" in English goes nowhere near the intensity of the meaning. "Moron" is the closest we can come. He calls them "morons"; they have no excuse whatsoever, since they had been properly trained and instructed for their role. They had brought shame to the whole occasion. The entire village would have felt insulted. It would be years before that village could hold up its head before neighboring villagers who would never cease to remind them of this disaster.

But notice, it is not the wise virgins who are used as the main point of the parable. They did what they were trained and expected to do, so there was no praise for them. Doing one's duty brings no rewards!

The morons in the parable are used by Jesus to make the point about the coming kingdom of God. When the groom shut the door after entering his new house, he was doing a most unusual thing. In those days doors were not shut on feasts: they were deliberately kept open in order to show that the honorable status of the participants had been more than maintained.

So why was the door shut for this feast? Passers-by and gapers would soon take note of the place of the missing bridesmaids. The shame they brought had to be shut off from public gaze. The bloodstained sheet would be displayed only to the official guests and not to the whole village. So great, you see, was the social effect of the one mistake these morons had created. This was not a matter of ignorance: they had been told exactly what to do. This was a mistake made out of stupidity and lack of attention to detail.

Thus Jesus used two kinds of women to make important points. Doing exactly what you are prepared for, in the way expected of you, brings no acclamation. Duty is done because it is expected. You need to exceed your duty to win any praise and honor, and that was almost impossible in Mediterranean society.

Also, doing your social duties ensured that the good order of your community would continue in peace and harmony. Duties and traditions were important to the Mediterranean world, far more important than laws, for they played a much more critical role in the maintenance of peace and prosperity.

The one failure of the five moronic virgins caused havoc to the entire community, not just in the wedding ceremony. Dishonor and shame were brought to the two families, and disruption to the life of the whole village.

Jesus' summary of the parable, "Watch therefore, for you know neither the day nor the hour," could be put like this: "See that you pay attention to even the slightest and least important detail of your life, for a failure in even the smallest detail will affect the good of everyone else in your community."

We are so individualistic in the way we now live our lives, relate to each other and serve God that this aspect of Jesus' parable escapes us.

Thus, Jesus uses two kinds of women to tells us very important things about our witness and service to God; and in doing so sets them outside their normal sphere—the home—to make his points.

The Woman Who Lost a Coin

"Or what woman, having ten silver coins, if she loses one coin, does not light a lamp and sweep the house and seek diligently until she finds it? And when she has found it, she calls together her friends and neighbors, saying, 'Rejoice with me, for I have found the coin which I had lost.' Just so, I tell you, there is joy before the angels of God over one sinner who repents."

(*Lk. 15:8-10*)

In this parable, Jesus sets the woman where she is expected to be—in her home. Unlike the setting of the previous parable, this was a poor woman. Her dowry was just ten drachmas—ten days wages of a worker. She had to look after her dowry for her husband, who was not allowed to spend it. It would be used to hand on to the husband of his eldest daughter. The dowry symbolized the social status of this family, and the whole village would have known how large or small it was.

She probably had the coins sewed into a kerchief, to be worn around her head on important days so her husband's honor could be displayed. To lose one was a disaster. So she swept the house from top to bottom, using up oil during the day to light her lamp so she could see into the dark corners where the coin could have rolled, until she found it and sews it back into its place.

She then called in her neighbors and friends and, as a woman would then have done, gone through the whole episode: showing them which coin had gone missing, how she had lit the lamp and swept the entire house out, and then showed them exactly where she found the coin. And notice, she admitted to having lost the coin.

This is the kind of bonding women do so well, ensuring the continuation of the social fabric of the community.

Men, of course, only celebrate their successes and good deeds: failures are never talked about. In the parable that precedes this one in Luke, there was a rich landowner who lost one of his hundred sheep. He left the ninety-nine in the care of his dogs and went off and found the lost one. When he returned he celebrated with his neighbors but he did not accept any blame for the sheep being lost.[5]

The honesty of this woman and her readiness to admit her faults before her friends is thus set in sharp contrast to the dishonesty of men in claiming only their successes and never admitting their faults in public.

Jesus leaves no doubt who will find a welcome in heaven.

The Widow Who Challenged a Judge

And he told them a parable, to the effect that they ought always to pray and not lose heart. He said, "In a certain city there was a judge who neither feared God nor regarded man; and there was a widow in that city who kept coming to him and saying, 'Vindicate me against my adversary.' For a while he refused; but afterward he said to himself, 'Though I neither fear God nor regard man, yet because this widow bothers me, I will vindicate her, or she will wear me out by her continual coming.'" And the Lord said, "Hear what the unrighteous judge says. And will not God vindicate his elect, who cry to him day and night? Will he delay long over them? I tell you, he will vindicate them speedily. Nevertheless, when the Son of man comes, will he find faith on earth?"

(Lk. 18:1-8)

Widows in Hebrew society, like orphans, were totally vulnerable, as I have already shown. They were not able to inherit their late husband's estate, and they would not be able to earn any income (other than in the street). They had no male to speak for them in the public courts or assemblies.

Thus widows become the symbol of the powerless, voiceless and oppressed.

In this parable, the judge is described as being shameless: he has no sense of the difference between what is sacred—belonging to God—and what is profane—what belongs to the people. For such a judge, the letter of the law is all that matters, no matter what the cost.

The widow had a legal problem, and with no man to go to court on her behalf, she was powerless and would lose out to her adversary. So she decided to go to his home and speak directly to him. This was outrageous in the extreme. She had no right to take such action, and any move on his part to even take notice of her would have brought him into great dishonor.

But she stuck to her guns and made herself so obnoxious that he had no option other than to take notice of her. Once having done that, he had to hold to the letter of the law and decide in her favor. Her outrageousness in going outside the bounds of her position in society brought its reward.

Jesus went on to point out that God is not like that judge. God does take immediate notice of all those who appeal for justice and vindicates them. And whereas the judge ended up being shamed by the persistence of the widow, God is honored by the speedy vindication of the oppressed.

Thus, three groups of women were used by Jesus in parables to show the kind of standards expected of all believers. In choosing women, Jesus was being quite outrageous in a day when women were valued only as adjuncts to men.

I now move on to those women who figure in the Acts of the Apostles to see whether the same trends continue in the life of the early church.

three

Women in the Acts of the Apostles

There were quite a few women who featured in the life and leadership of the first generation of Christians. I want to introduce them and show just how significant their contribution was.

The first mention of women in Acts occurred immediately after the ascension of Jesus. The eleven disciples returned to the upper room in Jerusalem where they "devoted themselves to prayer, together with [some] women and Mary the mother of Jesus, and with his brothers."[6]

This is the only mention of Jesus' mother outside the gospels. According to John's gospel, Mary had been taken out of her family and given over to the care and sponsorship of the apostle John,[7] thus taking away from Jesus' brother James the responsibility of caring for her. It is significant that when Luke wrote Acts, he separated Mary from Jesus' brothers, thus supporting John's gospel. The natural way of referring to them would have been something like "together with Jesus' brothers and his mother, Mary."

It is important to remember women were always identified in terms of their relationship to a male, whether husband, brother, son, uncle or cousin. A woman with no male relative to act as her sponsor was an embarrassment in this ancient society.

What is significant here, though, is that these women joined with the eleven apostles in prayer. This was unheard of in early Judaism, where women were invariably segregated from the men in the synagogues. That they took an active part in the prayer life of the early church was quite outrageous behavior and was, in fact, to become a sore point with Paul in Corinth.

When Peter later addressed the large meeting on the day of Pentecost, he addressed the men only.[8] This was because he was talking to Jews. The three thousand souls added to the church that day would have included the women and children of those men baptized. Luke specifies that women were being added to the Lord as well as men.[9]

The Widows of the Hellenists

> Now in these days when the disciples were increasing in number, the Hellenists murmured against the Hebrews because their widows were neglected in the daily distribution. And the twelve summoned the body of the disciples and said, "It is not right that we should give up preaching the word of God to serve tables. Therefore, brethren, pick out from among you seven men of good repute, full of the Spirit and of wisdom, whom we may appoint to this duty. But we will devote ourselves to prayer and to the ministry of the word." And what they said pleased the whole multitude, and they chose Stephen, a man full of faith and of the Holy Spirit, and Philip, and Prochorus, and Nicanor, and Timon, and Parmenas, and Nicolaus, a proselyte of Antioch. These they set before the apostles, and they prayed and laid their hands upon them.
>
> *(Acts 6:1-6)*

Sadly, language has been a great divider of people ever since God destroyed the human lust for divinity at the Tower of Babel. Among the early disciples of Jesus were those who spoke mostly Hebrew and those who spoke mostly Greek. The Hebrew-speaking disciples, led by Peter, seemed to have assumed they were superior and that those Hebrew-speaking women who had no male sponsors to care for them — generally called "widows" — should have the lionessess' share of the common fund.

Peter was not prepared to arbitrate on this. So he opted out by suggesting that the Greek-speakers should appoint seven men from their number to make sure the Greek-speaking widows would be properly cared for. What you see happening here is these seven men becoming the joint sponsors of these women, making sure they were adequately fed and clothed and housed. Here we see the separation of gospel preaching and social work—a trend that would continue until women forced a change.

What is important in this story is that these Greek-speaking widows no doubt made themselves heard and attracted the attention of the men to do something about the injustice and cultural prejudice that disadvantaged them. In doing that they went far beyond what society generally allowed them.

It is interesting to notice that the care of widows was the very first social service project undertaken by the fledgling church. Why widows? Because, as I have pointed out, such women with no extended family to take care of them were reduced to begging and often became prostitutes. Male orphans could find work, but not female orphans or widows.

This was the beginning of a new attitude where people were helped on the basis of their need rather than on the basis of maintaining the honor of the donors. As these women were to be fed, clothed and housed from resources provided by the common pool, there was no way anyone's name could be associated with any of this work.

When Saul started his persecution of the church, "he dragged off men and women and committed them to prison."[10] This is noteworthy, considering that he would not have bothered with women unless he felt they were a powerful force in the early church.

Sapphira

But a man named Ananias with his wife Sapphira sold a piece of property, and with his wife's knowledge he kept back some of the proceeds, and brought only a part and laid it at the apostles' feet. But Peter said, "Ananias, why has Satan filled your heart to lie to the Holy Spirit and to keep back part of the proceeds of the land? While it remained unsold, did it not remain your own? And after it was sold, was it not at your disposal? How is it that you have contrived this deed in your heart? You have not lied to men but to God." When Ananias heard these words, he fell down and died.

And great fear came upon all who heard of it. The young men rose and wrapped him up and carried him out and buried him.

After an interval of about three hours his wife came in, not knowing what had happened. And Peter said to her, "Tell me whether you sold the land for so much." And she said, "Yes, for so much." But Peter said to her, "How is it that you have agreed together to tempt the Spirit of the Lord? Hark, the feet of those that have buried your husband are at the door, and they will carry you out." Immediately she fell down at his feet and died. When the young men came in they found her dead, and they carried her out and buried her beside her husband. And great fear came upon the whole church, and upon all who heard of these things.

(Acts 5:1-11)

What was outrageous about Sapphira was she wanted to act as an equal partner with her husband, Ananias. And in that, she was accepted by Peter. But it entailed accepting her share of the responsibility of the pretense that the total proceeds of the sale of their land had been given to the common pool.

What was at stake in this incident was that Ananias and Sapphira wanted to have both the reciprocal honor of the outside community and the recognition of the Christian community for having given up a piece of land for the sake of those in need.

As land owners, they would have been required to give money to their local synagogue for the payment of scripture scrolls, furniture and scribes' stipends. In return their names would have been recorded as being attached to such gifts. Once they gave their assets away, they would have no more money with which to continue maintaining their honor in this way, and that would bring them the sneers of their neighbors. This was why they planned to retain some of the proceeds of the sale and continue to make their usual benefactions to the community and be honored and respected in return.

The problem with giving to the common congregational pool—laying the proceeds at the feet of the apostles—was that the donors' names became detached from particular gifts. There was also the situation that the gifts made from the common pool were based on the need of the recipients for help and not on the need for the donors to be honored. Since the recipients needed the money for basic sustenance they were in no financial position to respond by writing up the names of the donors—even if they knew them—on synagogue walls or on the notice boards of public buildings.

Thus Ananias and Sapphira wanted to continue to be respected and honored by their community for publicly recognized benefactions, and at the same time to be known by the Christian community as having given up their saleable assets for the support of the widows, orphans and anyone else in need. But, since there was only word-of-mouth recognition on the occasion of the donation, with no way of knowing who had received any of their money, Ananias and Sapphira—as with all those who gave their assets to the apostles—would not get any permanent public recognition for this.

These two were condemned for preferring the public honors of their community to the knowledge that their gift had saved a number of fellow believers from penury. This led them to pretend that what they had laid at the feet of the apostles was the total proceeds of the sale of their land.

In coming separately to the apostles to record her part in the donation, Sapphira was acting outside her role as wife. She wanted a separate recognition for her part in the donation rather than allowing her husband to take all the credit, as he was entitled to do in her society.

Having arrogated to herself such a status, she was also entitled to be judged separately. Thus, Sapphira paid the price of selfishly stepping outside her social position and of trying to hold on to her status in the community while pretending to be selflessly caring for the needy in her Christian community.

Mary the Mother of John (Mark) and Rhonda

When he realized this, he went to the house of Mary, the mother of John whose other name was Mark, where many were gathered together and were praying. And when he knocked at the door of the gateway, a maid named Rhoda came to answer. Recognizing Peter's voice, in her joy she did not open the gate but ran in and told that Peter was standing at the gate. They said to her, "You are mad." But she insisted that it was so. They said, "It is his angel!"

But Peter continued knocking; and when they opened, they saw
him and were amazed. But motioning to them with his hand to be
silent, he described to them how the Lord had brought him out of
the prison. And he said, "Tell this to James and to the brethren."
Then he departed and went to another place.

(Acts 12:12-17)

After Peter had been imprisoned by Herod following the popularity
Herod gained from the Jewish authorities after murdering James,
brother of John, some of the disciples met for prayer in the house of
Mary, mother of John (Mark).

This Mary is notable for two things: first because she did not sell
her house, give the proceeds to the twelve for the care of the poor and
then live off charity; the second because she allowed her house to be
used for Christian worship. She was the only person named for having allowed her house to be used in this way. While in Rome, Corinth
and other Roman cities outside Jerusalem there was no immediate danger in doing this, but in Jerusalem it was very dangerous. The Christians had to give up meeting in the temple and the synagogues because
of the persecution they suffered. Luke tells us there were some eight
thousand converts and that there was a steady increase in this number.

Where did these people meet, if not in the homes of those with
large enough areas to accommodate more than an average family?

Mary's decision to keep her home and use it in this way was in fact
a rather courageous one, risking both the ire of the Jewish authorities
and the criticism of other believers who thought she should have sold
it and shared her wealth with them.

Mary had a slave girl named Rhoda. That she continued to keep
her as a slave and not manumit her is significant, but it is obvious she
had begun to treat her as a human being. It was not until Paul enunciated the principle of deferring to each other that the institution of slavery began to be undermined, taking several centuries to disappear.

It is important to understand that Rhoda was a slave, not a paid
housemaid or servant. Most translators have been reluctant to use this
word because of the implication that Mary, mother of John (Mark)
and a believer, owned one or more slaves.

The institution of slavery was absolutely necessary for the stability of the economy of the Roman empire. Without slavery, the empire would have collapsed. The Hebrews continued to own slaves, as several of Jesus' parables indicate. Paul had things to say to Christian slave-owners to make them realize that one aspect of slavery—that a slave was an object to be possessed and not a person to be related to—must not apply to them.

Peter had been imprisoned for no specific crime by Herod Antipas, who had recently executed James, the brother of John. When Herod found that the Jewish temple bureaucracy really appreciated this disposal of the leader of the hateful Christians, he decided to capitalize on it and do the same with Peter, by then quite well known around the temple and the city. But Peter was released from prison by an angel of the Lord. So he went to where he knew some of the leaders were praying for him—the house of Mary.

When Rhoda was faced at the door with a Peter no longer in prison, she didn't stop to close the peephole and open the door to let him in, but rushed off and shouted to all those gathered for prayer that Peter was out of prison.

This gives us a clue that Mary was already treating her slave girl as a human being. Normally, Rhoda would have walked quietly up to her mistress and whispered the news to her. But, of course, being the word of a woman, and a slave in the bargain, her joyous outburst was not believed, so it was some minutes before the men took notice of Peter's continued knocking and went to let him in.

Thus Rhoda joins those women whose words were not believed because of her sex. But that did not stop her from telling her story and sticking to it, and being proved correct.

Tabitha

Now there was at Joppa a disciple named Tabitha, which means Dorcas. She was full of good works and acts of charity. In those days she fell sick and died; and when they had washed her, they laid her in an upper room. Since Lydda was near Joppa, the disciples, hearing that Peter was there, sent two men to entreat him, "Please come to us without delay." So Peter rose and went with them. And when he had come, they took him to the upper room. All the widows stood beside him weeping, and showing tunics and other garments which Dorcas made while she was with them. But Peter put them all outside and knelt down and prayed; then turning to the body he said, "Tabitha, rise." And she opened her eyes, and when she saw Peter she sat up. And he gave her his hand and lifted her up. Then calling the saints and widows he presented her alive. And it became known throughout all Joppa, and many believed in the Lord. And he stayed in Joppa for many days with one Simon, a tanner.

(Acts 9:36-43)

The management of finance and the organization of charity were always in the hands of men in that patriarchal society. It was some time before women were allowed to become equal with men in the practical service of the Christian congregations.

When we read Tabitha "was full of good works and doing acts of mercy," we need to understand that in this she was stepping outside what was considered the role of women in the congregations. What she was doing was different from those women in the gospels who accompanied Jesus and arranged food and accommodation for him and the twelve during their wanderings in Galilee. Tabitha was doing what so far only men had been commissioned to do: look after widows.

There is no indication why she did this work. We know from the next chapter that there was another disciple there, a man named Simon, a tanner; for it was on his roof that Peter had the vision that led him to Caesarea and Cornelius the centurion.

There can be no doubt, though, that the reason Peter brought Tabitha back to life was for the sake of the widows she took care of, and not for her sake.

Tabitha was the forerunner of many women who were to take their place in the congregations as caretakers of the widows and orphans.

Lydia

Setting sail therefore from Troas, we made a direct voyage to Samothrace, and the following day to Neapolis, and from there to Philippi, which is the leading city of the district of Macedonia, and a

Roman colony. We remained in this city some days; and on the
Sabbath day we went outside the gate to the riverside, where we
supposed there was a place of prayer; and we sat down and spoke
to the women who had come together. One who heard us was a
woman named Lydia, from the city of Thyatira, a seller of purple
goods, who was a worshiper of God. The Lord opened her heart
to give heed to what was said by Paul. And when she was baptized, with her household, she besought us, saying, "If you have
judged me to be faithful to the Lord, come to my house and stay."
And she prevailed upon us.

(Acts 16:11-15)

It is often forgotten that the Jewish synagogue was basically an organization of men: women were allowed in but had to worship separately.
When, in Philippi, Lydia led a group of women to meet for prayer
down by the river, she did so because what they were doing was tech-
nically not allowed to Jewish women without the leadership of men.
The riverside was where women went to do the family washing, so
there was hardly any likelihood of being seen by men.

There must have been very few Jewish household heads in Philippi. If there had been at least ten Jewish adult males, they would have
been required to meet as a synagogue for worship. It seems no such
synagogue meeting occurred in Philippi.

But Lydia was not Jewish. She had become attached to a Jewish
synagogue in Thyatira in Asia Minor as a "worshiper of God"—the
term used for non-Jews who attached themselves to a synagogue without actually converting to Judaism. As a gentile woman who had no
male sponsor—she was a single businesswoman—conversion was not
available to her. As there were probably a number of Jewish women
among this group, she led them down to the women's laundry by the
river on Sabbath days to join with some of the gentile women she had
encouraged to worship the Jewish God with her.

When Paul and Silas arrived and sat down with them to teach
about Jesus being the Messiah, she and the others stayed. This was
an unusual situation because women were not usually the recipients of
philosophy or religious teaching, especially in Judaism.

When she accepted Jesus as her Messiah, she called for her household slaves to join her in Christian baptism. That in itself was not unusual, for Luke has already written about the way the centurion Cornelius called for his family and slaves to join him in baptism under Peter. But it is Lydia's next reaction that is really outrageous. She turned to Paul and said to him, "If you have judged me to be faithful to the Lord, come to my house and stay." Luke reinforces the unusual nature of this request by adding, "And she *prevailed* upon us." The verb here has connotations of asking for something that is not according to custom or law.

As a single, unattached woman, Lydia was in a difficult position socially. She was a rich businesswoman and had plenty of money. She may have taken over the business from her husband after he died in war or a shipping tragedy. Inviting three single men to live in her house was not a socially acceptable thing for her to do. But she wanted to make some appropriate response to these men who had acted outside social custom by sitting down with her and her women friends and teaching them about the Messiah. This no doubt emboldened her to be equally outrageous and offer them accommodation in her house for some days.

I believe Lydia was a salutary lesson to Paul, forcing him to reexamine his own patriarchal attitude to women. It is also interesting that Paul's acceptance and encouragement of women in both Philippi and Thessalonica were often in sharp contrast to his attitude to women in Corinth and other cities. When Paul and Silas ran into trouble a little later in Thessalonica they had the support of "not a few of the leading women."

I have no doubt Paul had a great deal to thank the outrageous Lydia for during a stressful time in Macedonia.

Damaris

> But some men joined him and believed, among them Dionysius the Areopagate and a woman named Damaris and others with them.
>
> *(Acts 17:34)*

Paul found Athens, center of Greek life and culture, very unsettling. He was disturbed by the abundance of shrines and statues to Greek and Roman divinities that lined the streets of the city. In the market-place as he tried to proclaim Christ the son of the only true God, he kept coming up against pagan philosophers who laughed at him.

Word of the Jew with new ideas about Jesus and Anastasia—*anastasia* is the Greek word for resurrection, but Paul's superstitious listeners immediately took it to be the name of some new god—reached the ears of those whose responsibility it was to make sure all the philosophers who set up their schools in the city had been properly vetted. So they called upon Paul to give a guest lecture at their council meeting.

Paul tried very hard to get through to these highly educated but superstitious people. He used some of their own well-known philosophers and poets to show he was simply building on what had already been taught. But when they finally found that "Anastasia" was not the name of a new god but referred to the resurrection of Jesus, they cut him off before he had time to finish, promising to hear him at another time.

However, several people who were there did become believers. Luke names only two: Dionysius the Areopagate (who must have been one of the members of the council) and a woman named Damaris. Her name is a variant of "heifer" and suggests she was a high-class prostitute, especially since the only women who were allowed to attend the theater and meetings such as Paul had just addressed were courtesans. This would be why Luke does not name her father or any male sponsor, since to do so would have shamed them because of her profession. It would have taken a great deal of courage on her part to become a believer, especially as she may have been rather well-known, which was why Luke names her.

We never hear more of Damaris, and we do not hear anything about Athens again, either. Athens was not to play a significant part in the formation of the early church. Indeed it was some centuries before Athens would provide any significant Christian leadership at all.

Prisca

After this he left Athens and went to Corinth. And he found a Jew named Aquila, a native of Pontus, lately come from Italy with his wife Priscilla, because Claudius had commanded all the Jews to leave Rome. And he went to see them; and because he was of the same trade he stayed with them, and they worked, for by trade they were tentmakers.

(Acts 18:1-3)

After this Paul stayed many days longer, and then took leave of the brethren and sailed for Syria, and with him Priscilla and Aquila.

(Acts 18:18)

He began to speak boldly in the synagogue; but when Priscilla and Aquila heard him, they took him and expounded to him the way of God more accurately.

(Acts 18:26)

Luke draws attention to two Jews from Rome, Aquila and Priscilla, a husband-and-wife team of tent-makers who had been among those expelled from Rome. They had set up a tent-making business at Corinth. Paul joined them as a fellow craftsman. It was probably there that they became believers.

When Luke next mentions them, he calls them "Priscilla and Aquila." Luke uses the diminutive form of her correct name, "Prisca." By putting her name first, Luke is saying something about her development in the faith. He did the same thing when he sent them to Ephesus to teach Apollos the full Christian faith. For a woman to be involved in teaching a man, and to be a missionary at that, was indeed outrageous! Luke risked the ire of his readers by naming her first.

The Four Unmarried Daughters of Philip

On the morrow we departed and came to Caesarea; and we entered the house of Philip the evangelist, who was one of the seven, and stayed with him. And he had four unmarried daughters, who prophesied.

(Acts 21:8-9)

Philip was one of the seven elected by the Greek-speaking disciples among the Jerusalem congregations to look after the daily distribution to the Greek-speaking widows.[11] After the murder of Stephen he went into Samaria and won many to the Lord.[12] He was then sent by the Spirit toward Gaza where he baptized the Ethiopian eunuch.[13] From thence he went to Caesarea, where he must have married and settled down.[14]

For a man to have one unmarried daughter was considered an embarrassment; but to have four was unheard of! What was wrong with them that no husbands could be found for them?

The author of Acts tells us what their problem was: they were prophets.

I pointed out in citing the case of Anna[15] that women were not welcome as prophets. But Paul already had some experience with women exercising a prophetic ministry at Corinth.[16] Thus, while Philip would not have been honored in the general Caesarean community because of his four unmarried daughters, he was quite comfortable with having them exercise their prophetic ministry in the congregation that probably worshiped in his home.

It is easy for us to miss the force of Luke's comment on these daughters. Since he has identified Philip as one of the seven, why the necessity of mentioning the daughters unless there was something unusual about them? From the perspective of Theophilus, to whom Acts was addressed, the unmarried daughters needed to be accounted for in order to preserve the honor of their father.

Paul's Sister

This is the only mention of any member of the family of Paul of Tarsus (Acts 23:16). In this case it was his nephew who was credited with overhearing the plot to kill Paul as he was being transported from Jerusalem to Caesarea by the Roman authorities. Neither sister or nephew was named, even though Luke must have known them through his close relationship with Paul.

Who Paul's father was or how many siblings he had is never mentioned. All that can be deduced from this passage is that his sister was married and her son remained loyal to Paul, even though Paul had become a leading member of the group of Jews who had accepted Jesus as their Messiah and had thus earned the hatred of the leaders of the

Jewish temple in Jerusalem. It could well have been that after Paul's encounter with the risen Christ on the Damascus road and during the fourteen or so years he stayed in Tarsus, he persuaded his whole family to accept Jesus as Messiah.

The only other women named in Acts are two prominent women in the Roman administration.

Drusilla

She is named as the wife of Felix, procurator of Judea. She was in fact his third wife. Antonius Felix was himself a freedman, probably manumitted by Antonia, mother of the emperor Claudius. All we know of Drusilla is she was the daughter of Herod Agrippa I.

Bernice

She was the sister of Herod Agrippa II, governor of the region that included Caesarea, and was the elder daughter of Herod Agrippa I, who gave her in marriage to his brother Herod Philip. After her husband's death, she lived in her brother's house in a relationship that was claimed to be incestuous. She later married Polemon, king of Cilicia, the region in which Paul's city of Tarsus lay, but soon left him to return to her brother.

You can have some idea of what Paul's feelings were toward her when he saw her attend his trial before her brother Agrippa (Acts 25:13).

It can be seen that women played a very important part in the life of the early Christian church. Not only were they starting to take on some of the responsibilities for social work that were normally the domain of men, but they started to make their presence felt at the leadership level.

As I will show, this led to tensions as the church moved out into the Roman world. But it did not stop women from assuming responsibility under God for the day-to-day operations of the Christian congregations of which they felt they were equal members.

four

Women in Paul's Epistles

When you look at the people named in the epistles of the New Testament, you find a surprising number of women. This is unusual enough in itself, but, unless a married couple is referred to, all these women are named in their own right and not as being under the sponsorship of a male. This would have been quite unacceptable to both the Jewish and Greco-Roman societies of the time.

What we see here is the admittance of women into the world of males, and an acknowledgment that God overrode the social prejudices of the day.

Romans

The very first in a long list of people in Rome that Paul greets personally is

> ... our sister Phoebe; deacon of the church at Cenchreae, that you may receive her in the Lord as befits the saints, and help her in whatever she may require of you, for she has been a benefactor of many and of myself as well.
>
> *(Rom. 16:1-2)*

Phoebe may have delivered Paul's letter to the Roman church herself. This was unusual, and was probably because she was a rich benefactor in her own right at Cenchreae. Paul had no hesitation in breaking with custom and demanding she be treated according to her position in the community and not according to her sex. She joined those wealthy women who supported Jesus and his disciples with their money.

There is no evidence in the New Testament itself for an exact description of the role and function of a deacon. But what is certain is Phoebe is the only deacon named. She must have given outstanding service to the church at large to have become the only deacon named in the early church.

That Paul chose to name her as a deacon is a strong indication of the important leadership role played in the early congregations by women.

There is a very interesting inscription from the fourth century of our era, found at Jerusalem.

> Here lies the slave and bride of Christ, Sophia, deacon, the second Phoibe, who fell asleep in peace on the 21st month of March during the 11th indiction ... the Lord God ...[17]

Here is a fourth-century woman deacon being likened to first-century Phoebe; both are deacons and both are rich benefactors of the Christian community. This shows just how unusual Phoebe must have been in her day to have been remembered three hundred years later.

Prisca is next greeted. Paul always used her proper name, not the diminutive Priscilla, and placed her ahead of her husband Aquila, thus showing his great respect for her. He referred to the fact that she and her husband "risked their necks for my life, to whom not only I but also all the churches of the Gentiles give thanks." (Rom. 16:3-5)

They then had a house church meeting in their Roman home, so they were back there after the expulsion order on the Jews had been repealed. They also established a house church at Ephesus, where they had a great influence on the missionary Apollos.

Mary is noted as one who "worked hard among you" (Rom. 16:6). In this, she is being accorded the same status as any of the men who worked hard in Rome.

It is worth noting here that gospel work, whether evangelism or the building up congregations, was described as "manual labor"—this is the word for "work" Paul consistently used. In fact, most of the references to "work" in Paul's letters are about gospel work and not what we think of as manual labor.

Mary is thus one of the many women who worked side by side with Paul and his male coworkers in proclaiming the gospel of Christ. Her work was as exhausting and as crucial as was the men's.

Junia is probably the wife of Andronicus. The couple is described as "my kinsmen and fellow prisoners, people of note among the apostles, and they were in Christ before me" (Rom. 16:7). Junia is thus senior in the faith to Paul, something Paul would be rather reluctant to admit. The fact that he does ascribe Junia seniority in the faith is really an outstanding thing for a man like Paul who was brought up from childhood to believe a woman's place was in the home under the patronage of their father.

The fact that Paul does not name Junia as the wife of Andronicus is important, for it shows Paul accepted her in her own right and not just as the wife of Andronicus.

Tryphaena and **Tryphosa** are two women who are described also as "workers in the Lord" (Rom. 16:12). They could well have been sisters, even twins, as it was not unusual to give twins similar-sounding names. Tryphaena is also the name of a fictitious queen of Pisidian Antioch who showed kindness to Thecla in The Acts of Paul—a second-century romance.

Julia is probably the wife of Philologus (Rom. 16:15). Her name suggests a connection with Caesar's household.

The sister of Nereus is greeted. Nereus was a close friend of Flavia Domitilla, a Christian member of the Roman imperial family, who was banished to the island of Pandateria by her uncle Domitian in A.D. 95.

Thus, of those 28 greeted by name, eight are women—some 29 percent. This shows just how much Paul valued the work and leadership of women—despite the cultural sanctions against women playing leadership roles in either civic or religious life.

I Corinthians

Chloe is mentioned as the source of Paul's claim that there was much quarreling among the believers at Corinth (I Cor. 1:11). The phrase "Chloe's people" suggests she was the leader of a house church there or at Ephesus, from where Paul was writing. This is very important, for it means she may also have led the worship, even presiding at the Lord's Supper.

Prisca is again mentioned, this time as having a house church in Ephesus and having sent greetings with her husband Aquila to the believers at Corinth (I Cor. 16:19).

Philippians

Euodia and **Syntyche** are described as having "labored side by side with me in the gospel together with Clemens and the rest of my fellow workers, whose names are in the book of life" (Phil. 4:2-3). They are thus on equal footing with the men who worked with Paul at Philippi. Too often the disagreements between these two women are emphasized rather than the fact that they are accorded equal status with the men in the work of the gospel there. Their names are also in "the book of life," so Paul does not seem to want to waste too much energy resolving their problems. His main concern was that the work of the gospel in which they were all involved was not damaged in any way by the disagreements between them.

Colossians

Nympha is the head of a house church at Laodicea (Col. 4:15). She was another woman who probably presided at the Lord's Supper.

II Timothy

Paul reminds Timothy that both his grandmother **Lois** and his mother **Eunice** were in Christ before him. It is significant that neither the grandfather nor father rates a mention (II Tim. 1:5). Even if they were not believers, the fact they were not named is significant, because women were usually named as the daughter of, sister of, wife of or mother of a male.

An even more significant point is that Timothy's father was a Greek and not a Jew (Acts 16:1). According to Jewish tradition, Timothy was a Jew through his mother, which was why Paul insisted on circumcising him when he asked Timothy to join in his mission. Paul did not want Jews to use Timothy as proof that Paul was opposed to the law of Moses.

What is important here is that the Jewish tradition was being passed on to Timothy through his mother and grandmother; and when they became Christians through Paul, they continued Timothy's education in the gospel. In this, they risked the anger of the Greek community and of Timothy's father, since it was expected that Timothy would follow his father's profession, whatever that was.

Also of significance here was that these two women were responsible for teaching the faith to a male. In this they went outside the norms of both their own culture and their husband's culture. A mother traditionally took no further part in rearing male children once they reached puberty and became the responsibility of the father. Yet Timothy was reminded to take careful note of what these two women had taught him after he became a Christian, which would have happened in his adulthood.

These were two strong women of solid convictions who were prepared to be shamed by their local Greek community in order to make sure Timothy continued steadfastly in their newfound faith in Christ.

Prisca is again greeted (II Tim. 4:19), as is **Claudia** (II Tim. 4:21).

Philemon

Apphia is greeted as "our sister" and is a member of the house church of Philemon (Philem. II).

It is interesting to note that Paul referred to Apphia as "our sister," while the others named were called "fellow workers," "fellow soldiers" and "fellow prisoners."

Paul often made a distinction between those who worked with him in his mission and those who were members of established congregations. In this case, Apphia was a member of the congregation that met in the home of Philemon.

We have here an example of the church as the surrogate family of God, with Jesus as the elder brother and everyone else his siblings. No distinction was made between the male and female siblings for purposes of social status and leadership. It seems that in the early stages of the church, leadership was "gender neutral," to use a modern-day phrase.

There are no more women greeted or mentioned by name in the New Testament.

What comes through loud and clear is that in the early church women were included as equals within the leadership, ministering and missionary activities. Women were named as individuals in their own right, only being mentioned in association with a man when the husband is included. This was radical enough, let alone that women were shown as teachers, dispensers of charity and leaders of house churches. If the order of deacon is what is meant by the word "diakonos," then the only deacon named in the New Testament was a woman.

The respect thus shown to women served to set the early church apart, not only from its own secular community, but from the church of the second century onward.

- - - *five* - - -

Paul's Comments on Women

Whenever Paul comments on women in general and makes statements about their place in the congregations, we must always take into account the special circumstances and the context of the city and region involved. Too often what Paul said about women in a particular place has been universalized, as though Paul meant his words to apply to all women in all places for all time. A careful study of the problems Paul faced in each of these cities shows quite clearly that his comments about women and their place in the life and work of the church was dictated by the special circumstances he found in the church there. Often the power of the worship of a pagan goddess dictated the way women were looked upon in that region; this makes it even more important to take such things into consideration before quoting Paul's comments about women in a particular place and applying them uncritically and generally.

At Corinth

This Roman city had a worldwide reputation for its sexual licentiousness. The worship of Aphrodite was exceptionally strong at Corinth, resulting in temple prostitution. There were also a great number of street prostitutes, whose quarters can still be seen today among the Roman ruins. Sailors were keen to disembark at the two seaports of Corinth and sample the street girls.

It was also the case that women generally were denigrated there. Not one example of a woman in public office has come down to us from the early Roman period.

Bearing in mind that the Christians met in small groups in the homes of the wealthy, and that many of the women converts would have been ex-prostitutes, you must have some sympathy with Paul and his reluctance to bring the gospel into disrepute—as he saw it— by having ex-prostitutes praying and testifying. But it was also the fact that women generally were disparaged in Corinth, so their taking part in congregational worship and teaching would have been inappropriate in Paul's mind.

It is the general attitude of the Corinthian men toward women, as well as the renown of Corinth as the acme for sex tourists of the day, that should be borne in mind when reading what Paul had to say about Corinthian women. It should be noted that he did not say these same things about women in any other city.

> The body is not meant for immorality, but for the Lord, and the Lord for the body. And God raised the Lord and will also raise us up by his power. Do you not know that your bodies are members of Christ? Shall I therefore take the members of Christ and make them members of a prostitute? Never! Do you not know that he who joins himself to a prostitute becomes one body with her? For, as it is written, "The two shall become one flesh." But he who is united to the Lord becomes one spirit with him. Shun immorality. Every other sin which a man commits is outside the body; but the immoral man sins against his own body. Do you not know that your body is a temple of the Holy Spirit within you, which you have from God? You are not your own; you were bought with a price. So glorify God in your body.
>
> *(I Cor. 6:13-20)*

Paul wrote this in answer to questions asked by members of the congregations at Corinth. Unfortunately for us, Paul did not repeat the actual question, so we have to try to work out what he was exactly being asked.

Bearing in mind that unmarried men were very much in the minority in the ancient world, what we have here was a question about the use of street prostitutes by married men. But what is strange about Paul's answer is that he treats it as a religious issue and not a moral issue. He could so easily have invoked the seventh commandment even though according to Jewish tradition the married man would not be committing adultery unless the prostitute was married, for adultery was a sin against the married man, not the woman. However, he would have been told about Jesus' restatement of the law, making it adultery for a married man to have intercourse with an unmarried woman. The Jews among the Christian leaders in Jerusalem were very concerned about the lax morality of the gentile world and so would have been careful to tell Paul about what Jesus had said. And he certainly could have appealed to the various Christian sanctions against sexual promiscuity.

Instead, Paul treated this as a religious problem.

What is known is that the street prostitutes of Corinth looked to Aphrodite as their patron, even if they did not serve as temple prostitutes. To such a prostitute, having sex with a stranger was in some way an act of service to Aphrodite.

Paul is saying, then, that when a Christian man, who believed Christ's Spirit inhabited his body, was united with a prostitute who believed the spirit of Aphrodite inhabited her body, the overall mystical effect was that Christ was having sex with Aphrodite. He emphasized this by pointing out, referring to the second chapter of Genesis, that sexual intercourse is not just a pleasurable experience, like eating; but is an act that joins the man and the woman in a spiritual way.

Our Western notions of individuality and love-based sex were almost unknown in the Roman world. Marriage for love and commitment was rare. Marriage was a social institution for the procreation of children and the regulation of women. For a Roman man to have sex with a prostitute was not seen as threatening to the institution of marriage. He would have seen that as his right; but would, at the same time, instantly divorce his wife should she have sex with anyone else.

Thus, in this passage, Paul was not being harsh on women as women. Indeed, he accorded them a right to have their own experiences. The problem, as he saw it, was these prostitutes believed they were serving Aphrodite and at the moment of intercourse were representing her, giving the man the experience of mating with the god. No matter that the men could claim that, as Christians, they knew the pagan gods had no objective existence and so Aphrodite did not exist and thus they were having sex only with the prostitute.

Paul was more concerned with the perceptions of the non-Christian prostitute, the effect it would have on her and how she would then perceive Christian men who continued to use prostitutes. He was also concerned for those prostitutes who became Christians and how they would feel when they saw male members of their congregation resorting to prostitutes.

In Paul's view, each believer's body was a temple of Holy Spirit, and that temple should not be polluted by introducing pagan presences into it.

Now concerning the matters about which you wrote. It is well for a man not to touch a woman. But because of the temptation to immorality, each man should have his own wife and each woman her own husband. The husband should give to his wife her conjugal rights, and likewise the wife to her husband. For the wife does not rule over her own body, but the husband does; likewise the husband does not rule over his own body, but the wife does. Do not refuse one another except perhaps by agreement for a season, that you may devote yourselves to prayer; but then come together again, lest Satan tempt you through lack of self-control. I say this by way of concession, not of command. I wish that all were as I myself am. But each has his own special gift from God, one of one kind and one of another.

To the unmarried and the widows I say that it is well for them to remain single as I do. But if they cannot exercise self-control, they should marry. For it is better to marry than to be aflame with passion.

To the married I give charge, not I but the Lord, that the wife should not separate from her husband (but if she does, let her remain single or else be reconciled to her husband)—and that the husband should not divorce his wife.

To the rest I say, not the Lord, that if any brother has a wife who is an unbeliever, and she consents to live with him, he should not divorce her. If any woman has a husband who is an unbeliever, and he consents to live with her, she should not divorce him. For the unbelieving husband is consecrated through his wife, and the unbelieving wife is consecrated through her husband. Otherwise, your children would be unclean, but as it is they are holy. But if the unbelieving partner desires to separate, let it be so; in such a case the brother or sister is not bound. For God has called us to peace. Wife, how do you know whether you will save your husband? Husband, how do you know whether you will save your wife?

Only, let every one lead the life which the Lord has assigned to him, and in which God has called him. This is my rule in all the churches. Was any one at the time of his call already circumcised? Let him not seek to remove the marks of circumcision. Was any one at the time of his call uncircumcised? Let him not seek circumcision. For neither circumcision counts for anything nor uncircumcision, but keeping the commandments of God. Every one should remain in the state in which he was called. Were you a slave when called? Never mind. But if you can gain your freedom, avail yourself of the opportunity. For he who was called in the Lord as a slave is a freedman of the Lord. Likewise he who was free when called is a slave of Christ. You were bought with a price; do not become slaves of men. So, brethren, in whatever state each was called, there let him remain with God.

(I Cor. 7:1-24)

I have included this entire section because the question of wives and fiancées has to be seen within the context of the actual question being asked.

It seems one of the problems Paul faced here and elsewhere was the reaction of many Romans and Greeks to their conversion. Paul often used the imagery of freedom from slavery to explain the process of redemption through Christ. Once they were the slaves of sin. Satan was their master and he refused to release them—manumit them. Christ, by his death and resurrection, has freed them—manumitted them—from ownership by Satan and he has become their master. They are now, like Paul, the slaves of Christ. Redemption, as proclaimed by Paul, was an exchange of ownership, not a freeing from one owner to be a freedman.

Many converts, it appears, inferred that this process of being freed from slavery to Satan also involved the automatic severance from all the contractual relationships that controlled them in their pagan lives. A married man believed his conversion automatically ended his marriage and he was free from all family responsibilities. If he was an actual slave in bondage to a master, he believed he was no longer a slave and could simply walk away as though he had become a freedman. This resulted in a great deal of social chaos in Corinth.

Paul's corrective to this problem was to state this important principle: your redemption in Christ changed nothing in your social status and responsibilities. If you were married, you were to stay married and continue your family duties, but hopefully in a more just and loving way. If you were a slave, you stayed a slave, but served your master in a way deserving of your new master, Christ.

In looking at women and marriage here, it is important to understand that Paul was dealing with a specific problem and not with generalities. He was dealing with the situation when one partner in a pagan marriage became a Christian believer. Paul was not addressing the question of deciding whom to marry. Should a wife become a Christian believer, she was not to withhold sex from her husband; nor should the husband if he was the one who converted. Abstinence from sex is for religious purposes only and is to be decided mutually.

If there is a decision to separate, it is the non-Christian who decides. If the unconverted husband or wife decides to stay in the marriage, the Christian is obliged to agree and continue in the hope that the other partner will eventually become a Christian too.

It is important to state here that this passage is not about a Christian believer deciding whether or not to marry a nonbeliever. Paul deals with that elsewhere. He does suggest that widows and single women who become believers stay single, probably on the grounds that there would not be suitable single, believing men available. However, this needs to be tempered with an understanding of the problem single unattached women in the ancient world had in trying to survive without a male sponsor. One of the reasons many young widows turned to prostitution was because that was the only work available to them since people were reluctant to employ single women with no family connections. Paul had to face that problem later in his letters to Timothy.

The principle of staying in the social level of your pre-Christian life also applied to those who had been Jews. They were not to try to surgically undo their circumcision. Those who came to Christ as non-Jews were not to undergo circumcision since Christianity was not a sect of Judaism.

This whole section must be understood in the light of the actual question Paul was being asked, based on the cases of individuals within a marriage who were coming to Christ and whether that should automatically end the marriage.

We need to remember that marriage was primarily a contract between two families, not a lifelong commitment based on love. Vows of constancy and permanency are very much a Christian concept. Loving and caring for one's partner are also later Christian concepts. Paul was dealing with marriage as he found it in Roman cities. In Corinth, women were very much seen as sex objects and breeders of children. This meant that marriage as a Christian concept would have been much harder to teach there.

> Now concerning the unmarried, I have no command of the Lord, but I give my opinion as one who by the Lord's mercy is trustworthy. I think that in view of the present distress it is well for a person to remain as he is. Are you bound to a wife? Do not seek to be free. Are you free from a wife? Do not seek marriage. But if you marry, you do not sin, and if a girl marries she does not sin. Yet those who marry will have worldly troubles, and I would spare you that. I mean, brethren, the appointed time has grown very short; from now on, let those who have wives live as though they had none, and those who mourn as though they were not mourning, and those who rejoice as though they were not rejoicing, and those who buy as though they had no goods, and those who deal with the world as though they had no dealings with it. For the form of this world is passing away.
>
> I want you to be free from anxieties. The unmarried man is anxious about the affairs of the Lord, how to please the Lord; but the married man is anxious about worldly affairs, how to please his wife, and his interests are divided. And the unmarried woman or girl is anxious about the affairs of the Lord, how to be holy in body and spirit; but the married woman is anxious about worldly affairs, how to please her husband. I say this for your own benefit, not to lay any restraint upon you, but to promote good order and to secure your undivided devotion to the Lord.

If anyone thinks that he is not behaving properly toward his betrothed, if his passions are strong, and it has to be, let him do as he wishes: let them marry—it is no sin. But whoever is firmly established in his heart, being under no necessity but having his desire under control, and has determined this in his heart, to keep her as his betrothed, he will do well. So that he who marries his betrothed does well; and he who refrains from marriage will do better.

A wife is bound to her husband as long as he lives. If the husband dies, she is free to be married to whom she wishes, only in the Lord. But in my judgment she is happier if she remains as she is. And I think that I have the Spirit of God.

(I Cor. 7:25-40)

This is a continuation of the previous passage, but more heavily directed at marriage and betrothal. It should not be assumed that the "present distress" mentioned here is the imminent return of Christ. Paul was writing eighteen months or so after his first visit to Corinth in response to some questions he had been sent. He referred earlier to the dissension among the believers there, probably fomented by the false teachers and apostles who had arrived to undermine his authority.

Also, Paul's two-year residence at Corinth had shown him just how much the Corinthians lived for the moment. "Eat, drink and be merry for tomorrow we die" was very typical of their attitude to life. Everything, as in our modern world, was present-driven. Planning and forethought were for philosophers only.

In contrast, Paul indicated that Christian believers were future-driven. Forethought was essential to the Christian life. People were to marry, not just for the facility of regular sex, but to achieve some future purpose and some solidarity in their lives. This was probably the first time marriage had been presented as having a purpose outside of itself. Marriage is a vocation, a career, and should be treated with the same respect as any other career. This was in marked contrast to the rather cavalier attitudes toward marriage in the Corinth of that day.

For Christian women it meant that they were to be treated as human persons with rights and privileges, not as sexual objects. The marriage bond was to be treated seriously and not broken on a whim. For women, remarriage was to be very carefully thought about, especially since, at this early stage of the development of Christianity, there would have been a shortage of eligible unmarried Christian men.

The comments about the husband spending so much time and energy pleasing his wife instead of in Christian service should be seen within the context of a mixed marriage. So few single Christian men and women were available for marriage that mixed marriage was inevitable. Fathers of unmarried daughters had to maintain their honor and dignity by finding them suitable husbands. Unmarried men were laughed at, so they, too, needed to find suitable wives.

Where both husband and wife were Christian, the problem of balancing their marriage and their service to Christ was not nearly so critical, for many of the social conventions associated with pagan preconceptions of rights and duties of husbands to wives and vice versa would disappear when both partners were Christians.

So Paul's comments should be seen in the light of mixed marriages and not where both partners were Christians.

The problem of engaged couples is best understood as a mixed relationship where the husband-to-be was a Christian and his fiancée was not. Paul emphasized the permanency of Christian marriage, reminding the man that if he does not think his wife-to-be capable of handling a Christian marriage, he should end the relationship now rather than try it out and then face divorce.

Paul was thus just as concerned about the woman who, if divorced, would have a most difficult time surviving. It would be much better for her if her fiancé broke off the engagement.

But I want you to understand that the head of every man is Christ, the head of a woman is her husband, and the head of Christ is God. Any man who prays or prophesies with his head covered dishonors his head, but any woman who prays or prophesies with her head unveiled dishonors her head—it is the same as if her head were shaven. For if a woman will not veil herself, then she should cut off her hair; but if it is disgraceful for a woman to be shorn or shaven, let her wear a veil. For a man ought not to cover his head, since he is the image and glory of God; but woman is the glory of man. (For man was not made from woman, but woman from man. Neither was man created for woman, but woman for man.) That is why a woman ought to have a veil on her head, because of the angels. (Nevertheless, in the Lord woman is not independent of man nor man of woman; for as woman was made from man, so man is now born of woman. And all things are from God.) Judge for yourselves; is it proper for a woman to pray to God with her head uncovered? Does not nature itself teach you that for a man to wear long hair is degrading to him, but if a woman has long hair, it is her pride? For her hair is given to her for a covering. If anyone is disposed to be contentious, we recognize no other practice, nor do the churches of God.

(I Cor. 11:3-16)

Sexual identity was extremely important in the Roman world because of the growth of homosexuality and cross-dressing.

This was mirrored in the Old Testament world where marriage, during the wandering in the wilderness, was pretty much an instant affair. A young man came across a young girl in the field and, if she was from a suitable family, he could take her into his tent and make her his wife by having sexual intercourse with her. Imagine his chagrin if he carried her off and then discovered "she" was a man dressed as a woman!

Also, there was a pressing need for Israel to populate as quickly as possible, especially with males, since there were wars to be fought. Any practice that prevented any act of sexual intercourse from resulting in pregnancy was proscribed.

But there was also the problem of the way Corinthian prostitutes were dressed in order to be recognizable as prostitutes. No respectable Roman matron wanted to be propositioned by a drunken sailor.

From studying designs painted on Corinthian pots and created in mosaics, it seems to me the way the prostitutes did their hair was the main way of displaying their trade. With their hair cut and decorated in outlandish ways, these women immediately attracted the attention of their potential customers.

Now think about any of these women who became Christian believers. It would take some time for their hair to grow out and look normal. One solution was to shave off their hair and wait for it to grow back normally. But this caused problems, since adulteresses often were forced to have their hair shaved off and go bareheaded to atone for the disgrace they brought upon their husbands.

Paul was concerned about those men who wandered around from congregation to congregation. (The word "angel" here need not refer to a heavenly messenger. Being sexless beings they were not likely to understand human sexuality, let alone be offended by it.) As they surveyed the women in these small groups, they could easily distinguish those who had once been prostitutes or who had been clean-shaven for adultery. Paul's answer to this problem was to invoke a Jewish custom that required women to wear a veil while at worship. If all women wore a veil over their heads, none of the men could distinguish those who had been prostitutes and those who had not. In a highly sensual society like Corinth, it was important to reduce the sexual undertones of congregational meetings as much as possible. Visiting men wondering about the presence of a prostitute they may well have used would not engender the kind of worshipful attitudes Paul had in mind.

Again, sexual identity and the social roles that go with it were important to Paul's principle that conversion changed nothing in society generally. Men were not to wear long hair or wear veils. Women were not to wear short hair and remain bareheaded.

Much has been made of Paul's "headship" argument in this passage. What must be continually borne in mind is the general perception that Corinthian men had of their womenfolk. In a society where women were playthings, sex objects and of no status value at all, it was necessary for change to proceed slowly. It would take a generation or two of Christianity for women to become respected human beings. Paul obviously felt the best way for Christian women to make a mark in the church and in the community was to act appropriately as wives, daughters and mothers. In this way they could build up respect for their sex and engender a whole new basis for their relationships in society.

It is also important to understand that the word "head" is not being used as "chief executive officer" here. It is being used in its primary meaning as "source" or "coordinator." While the husband is still the focus of the identity and honor of the family, he should not act as though he was the dictator, expecting instant and unquestioning obedience from his wife.

The wife was to play a responsible and responsive part in marriage, not imagining her conversion had somehow freed her from her marriage contract.

This whole section must be read as a unity and not as separate and separable units. Within the surrogate family of God that is the church, Paul was stating quite clearly that males and females—the brothers and sisters of their elder brother Christ—are equal in status. The long and involved argument about who was created first and who reflects the glory of God directly boils down to this one proposition, "Nevertheless, in the Lord woman is not independent of man nor man of woman; for as woman was made from man, so man is now born of woman. And all things are from God" (v.11).

Women are to be accorded a dignity and a place in Christian society that runs counter to the very low status given them in Corinthian society.

> As in all the churches of the saints, the women should keep silence in the churches. For they are not permitted to speak, but should be subordinate, as even the law says. If there is anything they desire to know, let them ask their husbands at home. For it is shameful for a woman to speak in church. What! Did the word of God originate with you, or are you the only ones it has reached?
>
> *(I Cor. 14:33-36)*

Here, "in all the churches of the saints" should not be universalized as though all Christian congregations around the Roman world and in Jerusalem had this as their rule. You have only to read Paul's letter to the Philippian congregations to understand this was not the case, for he commends women for their ministry. I have no doubt Paul was referring to all the gatherings of Christian believers in the Roman province of Achaia, an area that covered a great deal more than the actual capital, Corinth, itself. It must not be imagined that the city of Corinth was the only place in Achaia Paul visited and established congregations. He most probably journeyed to several of the towns and villages in the vicinity, wanting to meet up with the families of those who had come to Corinth for their weekly shopping, heard him and had been converted. He would have wanted to help them set up their own house churches. And, also, at this early stage in their development, Christian congregations were not aware of what was happening elsewhere in the world.

We can have no idea at all what actually provoked Paul's outburst against Corinthian women here. All we need to remember is Paul encouraged the full participation of women in his own missionary work and in congregations outside Corinth. We also need to remember that the only woman deacon named in the New Testament came from Cenchreae, a major seaport of Corinth.

This is not a general prohibition against all Christian women to remain silent in church.

In Galatia

The region of Galatia Paul visited was known as being wild, even in its day. There were many dialects spoken there, and many races. The ancient Celts were a strong presence. Paul had come to understand that it was a very multicultural area, with Greeks not necessarily in the majority. He had to come to terms with a great number of different religions and philosophies being practiced and taught there.

You have only to read about his experiences in this part of the world to appreciate the problems he must have had with the few Christian congregations that arose there (Acts 13 and 14).

His letter to the various congregations scattered around Galatia is a careful statement of the basic Christian doctrines, taking note of some of the main heresies that were starting to creep in.

> Now before faith came, we were confined under the law, kept under restraint until faith should be revealed. So that the law was our custodian until Christ came, that we might be justified by faith. But now that faith has come, we are no longer under a custodian; for in Christ Jesus you are all sons of God, through faith. For as many of you as were baptized into Christ have put on Christ. There is neither Jew nor Greek, there is neither slave nor free, there is neither male nor female; for you are all one in Christ Jesus. And if you are Christ's, then you are Abraham's offspring, heirs according to promise.
>
> *(Gal. 3:23-29)*

This is a clear enunciation by Paul of the principle
related directly to God through Christ as individu
structed by their society. No matter how a societ
and status of its tribes, races and sexes, God reco;
at all and treats every person as a sibling of Christ.

If the status of males and females in Christ is of social equals, that
should have brought about a revolution in the place of women in the
Christian congregations. Sadly, it did not happen, even though Paul, in
the way he used women as equal members of his missionary teams,
tried to set the standard. But social attitudes passed on from parent to
child over many generations do not go away overnight.

For women, Paul's dictum did not mean they had to become men
in order to become "sons of God." (There is a strange passage in the
Gospel of Thomas [logion 114] where Jesus talks about Mary Magdalene having to become a man before she can be acceptable.) Nor did
it mean they had to disregard their social roles and responsibilities.

The insistence by Paul in other letters that husbands treat their
wives by loving them as themselves was a sure way of breaking down
the oppressed situations of women in marriage. But like his direction
to treat slaves as equals, this did not lead to a revolution in women's
roles for a thousand or more years. Paul seems intent on preserving the
overall social relationships while at the same time challenging Christians to adopt different attitudes within those roles.

Sadly, Paul's dictum about all being one in Christ has never to this
day been fulfilled to the letter in any Christian denomination.

At Ephesus

Ephesus was the virtual capital of Asia and Asia Minor. It had been
given a great deal of independence by Rome and was the center of com-
merce and trade for the whole of the Roman province of Asia.

The worship of Artemis was the key to understanding the social
importance of women in Ephesus. By this time, Ephesus had become
the headquarters of the cult of Artemis; the statue and temple there
were one of the wonders of the ancient world. Artemis was the guardian of virginity and motherhood. Artemis, twin of Apollo, was a powerful divinity, resulting in the elevation of women socially in Ephesus.

at we have here is the opposite of what happened in Corinth, where he worship of Aphrodite resulted in depravity, especially of women.

In Ephesus, men married to enhance their social status. Husbands were noted for the way they lavished their wives with slaves and apparel. The reputation of a husband could be made or broken by the way his wife made her appearances in public.

This aspect of Ephesian life must be kept in mind when reading what Paul has to say about the roles of husbands and wives.

> Be subject to one another out of reverence for Christ. Wives, be subject to your husbands, as to the Lord. For the husband is the head of the wife as Christ is the head of the church, his body, and is himself its Savior. As the church is subject to Christ, so let wives also be subject in everything to their husbands. Husbands, love your wives, as Christ loved the church and gave himself up for her, that he might sanctify her, having cleansed her by the washing of water with the word, that he might present the church to himself in splendor, without spot or wrinkle or any such thing, that she might be holy and without blemish. Even so husbands should love their wives as their own bodies. He who loves his wife loves himself. For no man ever hates his own flesh, but nourishes and cherishes it, as Christ does the church, because we are members of his body. "For this reason a man shall leave his father and mother and be joined to his wife, and the two shall become one flesh." This mystery is a profound one, and I am saying that it refers to Christ and the church; however, let each one of you love his wife as himself, and let the wife see that she respects her husband.
>
> *(Eph. 5:21-33)*

Children, obey your parents in the Lord, for this is right. "Honor your father and mother" (this is the first commandment with a promise), "that it may be well with you and that you may live long on the earth." Fathers, do not provoke your children to anger, but bring them up in the discipline and instruction of the Lord.

Slaves, be obedient to those who are your earthly masters, with fear and trembling, in singleness of heart, as to Christ; not in the way of eye-service, as men-pleasers, but as servants (slaves) of Christ, doing the will of God from the heart, rendering service with a good will as to the Lord and not to men, knowing that whatever good anyone does, he will receive the same again from the Lord, whether he is a slave or free. Masters, do the same to them, and forbear threatening, knowing that he who is both their Master and yours is in heaven, and that there is no partiality with him.

(Eph. 6:1- 6:9)

Unfortunately in many editions of the New Testament the opening verse, "Be subject to one another out of reverence for Christ," is separated off from what follows by a subheading, leading to a misunderstanding of what Paul is actually teaching.

Christians are to defer to each other in Christ, and this is to be the guiding principle in all their social relationships as Christians. Paul then spells out what this means for three sets of relationships: husbands and wives, parents and children, masters and their slaves.

In each case, each partner is to defer to the other. This means there is no ruling partner with absolute control over the other. There is no partner socially superior to the other by virtue of the marriage. This, in effect, served to break down the oppressive rule of husband over wife, father over children and master over slaves. The social structures remained, but the attitudes of the partners within the structures were completely revolutionized.

How then was a wife to defer to a husband while at the same time the husband was to defer to the wife?

In the case of the husband he was to love his wife—be totally committed to her welfare—in the same sacrificial way Christ loved—was totally committed to—the church. This meant putting her and her needs ahead of his. This was a total reversal of the way husbands generally behaved in Asia Minor at the time. Not only did the husband have absolute right over his wife; he also married her, as I have already pointed out, in order to advance his own social status. The rich husbands always provided their wives with costly and fashionable clothing and many slaves—but in order to advance their own standing in the community. Bystanders would say, "Look how Cornelius dresses his wife—look at all those household slaves that accompany her! Isn't he a great man!" In this way the husband's own ego was being fed; it did not mean he really cared about his wife for her own sake.

I would interpret Paul's words in this way:

Now look here you husbands! Now that you are Christians you must stop treating your wives as status objects. Up until now you considered only yourselves and the esteem others gave you because of your wife. But now as a Christian husband you must put your wife's personal interests above your own. You must be genuinely committed to her welfare without a single thought of any kudos you may receive in return. You must be totally committed to her, not to yourself. You must love her sacrificially as Christ loved the church. You must give yourself to your wife and give up all notions of self-interest and status.

Paul's words to these men of Asia Minor would have struck terror into their hearts. Defer to their wives? Look after their welfare for their own sakes?

In return—and this is the key—in return for this self-sacrificing commitment to her, the wife was to obey her husband in the knowledge that what he would ask of her would be no different from what Christ asked of him.

What we have here is almost, but not quite, conditional obedience. The wife's obedience is based upon the husband's commitment to her. What so often happens today is that men will point to the need for his wife's obedience to him without at the same time acknowledging her right to his self-sacrificing on her behalf. Mutual deference means mutual submission; and this mutuality is based upon the equality of both parties in Christ.

"Headship" here is clearly about source and not structural authority. Christ is the source of the church, having died and been raised to found the church, giving birth to individual believers. So the husband is the founder of the family, being the one who invited his wife to join him in this partnership. He then fathers children in that marriage and is thus the source of that family. And as Christ is the self-sacrificing founder of the church, so is the husband the self-sacrificing founder of his family. There is no question here of the wife being the junior partner in Christian marriage.

The same logic then flows on to the relationship between father and children. In that society children had no status at all. The eldest son took over the status of head of the family only at the death of his father. Underaged children had no status or rights at all.

This means Paul's call for fathers to defer to their children by not provoking them through demanding total and unthinking obedience was a turning upside-down of family values. When fathers defer to their children in this way, then children are to defer to their father's will because they will know that what is being asked of them is for their own good. They would be glad to honor such fathers.

Again, family structures have not been interfered with. The family will look like any other family except the attitudes of the members to each other will be rather different.

The same process occurs with masters and slaves. Each is to defer to the other, with the obedience of the slave being prompted by the caring attitude of the masters. The other important thing here is Paul does not distinguish between male and female slaves. In the Roman world female slaves were treated very differently from male slaves. For Paul, sex differences did not apply: *all* slaves were to be treated with respect.

It is important to remember the Asia Minor context in which this letter was written, whether by Paul or by someone writing in his name. No attempt should be made to universalize this material without first taking the context into account and then allowing for the effect of other contexts on the principles Paul was applying.

> I desire then that in every place the men should pray, lifting holy hands without anger or quarreling; also that women should adorn themselves modestly and sensibly in seemly apparel, not with braided hair or gold or pearls or costly attire but by good deeds, as befits women who profess religion. Let a woman learn in silence with all submissiveness. I permit no woman to teach or to have authority over men; she is to keep silent. For Adam was formed first, then Eve; and Adam was not deceived, but the woman was deceived and became a transgressor. Yet woman will be saved through bearing children, if she continues in faith and love and holiness, with modesty.
>
> *(I Tim. 2:8-15)*

Writing some years later to Timothy who was then in Ephesus looking after the congregations there on his behalf, Paul continued with his concern for women that they not step outside the structural role of their society, while at the same time engendering Christian attitudes in their lives.

They were accustomed to dress and decorate their hair in order to add to the status and honor of their husbands. Paul was asking them to dress and have hairstyles that drew attention to the modest way of life befitting the wife of a husband who put Christ and not himself as the head of his family.

The role of wife in Ephesus, given the social context, was best expressed in child-rearing rather than as a society showpiece, or as trying to outdo her husband socially by pretending to have authority over him.

Here, as at Corinth, the pagan worship was dominated by a female god; but in this case it was Artemis, who was associated not so much with sexual license as with birth and motherhood.

Paul's interpretation of the Genesis account of the fall is inconsistent with the narrative itself, which makes it quite plain that Adam himself was there with Eve during the temptation by the serpent, and that he acquiesced. What we are to make of this for today is a difficulty I do not think has yet been satisfactorily resolved.

> The women likewise must be serious, not slanderers, but temperate, faithful in all things.
>
> *(I Tim. 3:11)*

Who were these women? Were they female deacons or wives of deacons? The Greek word for "wife" is the same as the word for "woman." There is no difficulty with them being women deacons in the light of Phoebe. It is interesting here that women are not being asked to be subordinate to the men. But they are being asked to have the same attitudes as the men.

> Do not rebuke an older man but exhort him as you would a father; treat younger men as brothers, older women as mothers, younger women like sisters, in all purity.
>
> *(I Tim. 5:1-2)*

Bearing in mind that Timothy was not acting as a bishop in Ephesus, but as Paul's temporary representative, it is interesting to note that his structural authority is being tempered with his Christianity. In that society, the old men of the tribe were to be respected but not necessarily obeyed unquestioningly; the older brother did have authority over his younger siblings—male and female—and mothers were respected but secondarily to their husbands.

Paul was demanding of Timothy that he not pretend to a type of apostolic authority that demanded instant and unquestioning obedience, irrespective of social status. This gives us an important clue to the way Paul himself related to those congregations he founded during his missionary years. Although he claimed to have apostolic authority directly from the Risen Christ, he chose rarely to exercise it in any autocratic fashion.

This does mean Paul was rather different from the Roman and Greek religious authorities in the way he gave women their due place in the congregations.

Paul's words to Timothy are best understood within the context of the church being a surrogate family, with God as the father and Christ as the elder brother and all human members Christ's siblings, on an equal footing with each other.

> Honor widows who are real widows. If a widow has children or grandchildren, let them first learn their religious duty to their own family and make some return to their parents; for this is acceptable in the sight of God. She who is a real widow, and is left all alone, has set her hope on God and continues in supplications and prayers night and day; whereas she who is self-indulgent is dead even while she lives. Command this, so that they may be without reproach. If anyone does not provide for his relatives, and especially for his own family, he has disowned the faith and is worse than an unbeliever.
>
> Let a widow be enrolled if she is not less than sixty years of age, having been the wife of one husband; and she must be well attested for her good deeds, as one who has brought up children, shown hospitality, washed the feet of saints, relieved the afflicted, and devoted herself to doing good in every way. But refuse to enroll younger widows; for when they grow wanton against Christ they desire to marry, and so they incur condemnation for having violated their first pledge. Besides that, they learn to be idlers, gadding about from house to house, and not only idlers but gossips and busybodies, saying what they should not. So I would have

younger widows marry, bear children, rule their households, and give the enemy no occasion to revile us. For some have already strayed after Satan. If any believing woman has relatives who are widows, let her assist them; let the church not be burdened, so that it may assist those who are real widows.

(I Tim. 5:3-16)

The Roman world was replete with young widows because so many young husbands lost their lives in wars and skirmishes. The Roman army was the only police force throughout the empire and so took a great number of men away from the main cities.

The problem widows faced—especially younger ones with no male relatives to look after them—was their inability in that society to earn money; where younger widows refused to become sex workers, they had little to do with their time, and became a drain on the social work funds of congregations. With nothing to do they congregated in groups and caused trouble, bringing themselves and their congregations into disrepute.

Paul wanted a distinction to be drawn between real widows and those who had some family left to them. It was up to the families of widows to take them back into their homes and look after them, finding suitable husbands where possible. This latter was difficult in a day when virginity was still valued as the minimum requirement in a prospective wife. But widows with families were not to become dependent on the charity of congregations. Men who refused to look after widows in their own families were acting in a way dishonorable to Christ.

Only those widows with no family to look after them were to have any right to congregational support. This is pared down to widows no younger than 60 years of age who have proved themselves worthy of support by the way they have given themselves to their own families as wives and mothers. Younger widows must marry again and bring up their children in an unblemished Christian fashion.

Thus what is really at issue is "Which husbandless wives are to be defined as 'real widows' and are therefore to be cared for by the congregation?"

Here (I Tim. 9-16) is what Paul regards as the minimum qualifications for the category of widow worthy of congregational support:

- ≤ To be over sixty years of age. They would thus be well past childbearing, past sexual promiscuity and too worn out from family responsibilities to care for themselves.
- ≤ To have related to only one husband. To have had more than one husband provokes the idea of having been committed to more than one man and his extended family, of adapting to the needs of more than one man, or changing loyalties.
- ≤ To have demonstrated her commitment to her husband by bringing up his children to enhance his reputation.
- ≤ To have enhanced his reputation for hospitality, especially in serving Christians.
- ≤ To have enhanced his reputation by charitable works, works for the needy, and by doing good in every possible way.

If Paul seems to us rather harsh in his treatment of widows in Ephesus, we must read between the lines and see the extent of the problem there. He saw how undeserved charity was counterproductive. He wanted members of the congregations there to accept full responsibility for their families and help only those widows who were genuinely without family support and who could not contribute to society again by remarrying.

Now, why were widows a problem in Asia, but apparently not elsewhere in the Empire? It was a warring era, so there would have been a neverending supply of widows everywhere. But the extended family patterns of that era would have normally met that need. Why not, apparently, in Ephesus?

Bearing in mind the place of a woman in Ephesus, and that her sole role was to enhance her husband's position, you can see that a "husbandless wife" is a nonperson. Having no husband to live for, a widow had no place in that community. A widow had no value in herself: no status. And that was precisely the problem facing the church. Wives with no husbands could not possibly be accepted as individuals with rights to read the scriptures, pray, prophesy, teach and so on. The general community outside the church would not value a congregation composed of nonpersons. The Good News would be brought into disrepute if widows were involved in its work of proclamation.

This was totally in accord with Paul's strategy everywhere he went: he wanted nothing to be said or done that would devalue the Good News in the eyes of the unconverted. It was also quite clear that a prerequisite for consideration as a "real widow" was to have been a perfect wife. Only those who had demonstrated they had lived blamelessly in the eyes of the general community as the wife of the recently deceased could qualify as real widows and be recipients of the social caring of the congregation.

In no way can verses nine and ten be made to apply to what a husbandless wife had done during her widowhood. She would have needed to have been a "younger widow" to have achieved all that; and to lose her husband while still young was a wife who had not yet proven herself to be a "good wife." Thus she could not qualify as a "real widow."

The only path open for a young widow in Ephesus, therefore, was to marry again and start once more the process of becoming a "good wife." Should she again be widowed she would fail to qualify anyway, since she had been the wife of more than one husband.

Thus the minimum age of sixty refers to when her husband died, not the age she must reach as a widow before she could qualify for care.

Also notice that in first-century terms, sixty is rather old. A sixty-year-old woman would be physically worn out from all her family duties. Without servants—she needed a husband to keep servants— she would not be able to care for herself. She would be totally dependent on her family. If she had no family to care for her, she could claim the charity of her congregation. The idea that at age sixty she had to qualify for care by enrolling in a religious order of "widows" that looked after other people's children, tended to the clergy and the needy, was monstrous. It is totally out of keeping with the rest of the New Testament and its concerns that we love each other and minister to each other's needs.

A wife who lost her husband at age twenty-five or so was still full of energy. She could care for herself and her children, and earn a living, at least in theory. The problem in Ephesus was she was now a non-person: no one would employ her because she had no husband to whom the wages and kudos would go. She then became a drifter, her only friends being other younger widows, and a moral danger to all the young men around.

What the writer says in verses nine to fifteen merely reflects what was happening in the community because of the way it regarded young widows generally as nonpersons.

The sixty-year-old widow is past caring what people think. She was now the object of caring, not a potential caretaker.

In this area the church both accepted the reality of the community's mentality and also set a standard of caring where it mattered most.

This passage, then, was about who qualified for the total caring of the congregation in the matter of one particular category of need: a recently widowed woman over sixty with no close family to care for her in her few remaining years. And notice that the "real widows" are to be honored.

The next problem for Timothy was how to help those young wives at home with not too much to do, and thus at the mercy of wandering teachers and magicians who liked to take advantage of them.

> For among them are those who make their way into households and capture weak women, burdened with sins and swayed by various impulses, who will listen to anybody and can never arrive at a knowledge of the truth.
>
> *(II Tim. 3:6-7)*

False teachers were a problem very early on in the church, especially in Asia Minor where pagan mystery religions were rife and where there were several philosophers who tried to combine paganism with Christianity and create a mixture that horrified Paul.

Young women at home, not very well educated, with their husbands away on military service, were especially at risk from these unscrupulous people who used them for their own purposes without caring at all for them as individuals. While Paul seemed to be denigrating them, he was certainly concerned that they be helped into a better understanding of the faith, as well as playing a more constructively Christian part in home and family life.

Timothy needed to treat them as sisters and encourage them back to the true faith.

At Colossae

Wives, be subject to your husbands, as is fitting in the Lord. Husbands, love your wives, and do not be harsh with them. Children, obey your parents in everything, for this pleases the Lord. Fathers, do not provoke your children, lest they become discouraged. Slaves, obey in everything those who are your earthly masters, not with eyeservice, as men-pleasers, but in singleness of heart, fearing the Lord. Whatever your task, work heartily, as serving the Lord and not men, knowing that from the Lord you will receive the inheritance as your reward; you are serving the Lord Christ. For the wrongdoer will be paid back for the wrong he has done, and there is no partiality.

(Col. 3:18)

Masters, treat your slaves justly and fairly, knowing that you also have a Master in heaven.

(Col. 4:1)

This is a condensed version of Paul's household code to the Ephesians. Colossae was also in Asia Minor, and so set in much the same context as Ephesus.

In Crete

But as for you, teach what befits sound doctrine. Bid the older men be temperate, serious, sensible, sound in faith, in love, and in steadfastness. Bid the older women likewise to be reverent in behavior, not to be slanderers or slaves to drink; they are to teach what is good, and so train the young women to love their husbands and children, to be sensible, chaste, domestic, kind, and submissive to their husbands, that the word of God may not be discredited. Likewise urge the younger men to control themselves. Show yourself

in all respects a model of good deeds, and in your te
integrity, gravity, and sound speech that cannot b
that an opponent may be put to shame, having no
of us. Bid slaves to be submissive to their masters and to
isfaction in every respect; they are not to be refractory, nor to pil-
fer, but to show entire and true fidelity, so that in everything they
may adorn the doctrine of God our Savior.

For the grace of God has appeared for the salvation of all
men, training us to renounce irreligion and worldly passions, and
to live sober, upright, and godly lives in this world, awaiting our
blessed hope, the appearing of the glory of our great God and
Savior Jesus Christ, who gave himself for us to redeem us from
all iniquity and to purify for himself a people of his own who are
zealous for good deeds.

(Titus 2:1-14)

Titus was doing in Crete what Timothy was doing in Ephesus: representing Paul, not being a direct supervisor or leader of the congregations there.

This passage was an expansion of the household code as we saw
it in both Ephesus and Colossae. There was the same emphasis on preserving the social structures but injecting Christian attitudes into
them.

In particular, Paul was reinforcing the traditional role of the grandmother in the extended Roman family. She was the one who handed
on the culture and traditions. She trained the children, especially the females, in the home and family arts and crafts. She inducted them into
the mysteries of married life. Grandmothers also passed on the family
traditions to their grandsons, as for example in the case of Timothy,
whose grandmother Lois may have been responsible for his initial coming to faith in Christ.

Paul wanted all this to continue, but to include Christian ways,
traditions, attitudes and beliefs.

In summary, then, it can be seen that Paul was more than happy to have
women working alongside him in his mission to the gentiles. He invariably named them with a single name and not as the wife of, daughter

, sister of or niece of, some family male, as would have been expected in the Roman and Hebrew societies. He was careful to take into account the perceptions of women held by the local community so that no taint of scandal could fall upon the reputation of the gospel. He asserted their rights as individuals within family and community structures and was happy for them to have leadership roles when these did not conflict with the social values of the region.

Paul was, nevertheless, still somewhat patriarchal, tending to subordinate women to their menfolk. But it should be granted to him that he stepped far beyond the mores of his time and continued the process of freeing women to be full members of society, a process begun by Jesus.

six

Others' Comments on Women

Only two other writers in the New Testament make any comments about women and their place in the life of the Christian congregations.

Peter

Servants, be submissive to your masters with all respect, not only to the kind and gentle but also to the overbearing. For one is approved if, mindful of God, he endures pain while suffering unjustly. For what credit is it, if when you do wrong and are beaten for it, you take it patiently? But if when you do right and suffer for it you take it patiently, you have God's approval. For to this you have been called, because Christ also suffered for you, leaving you an example, that you should follow in his steps. He committed no sin; no guile was found on his lips. When he was reviled, he did not revile in return; when he suffered, he did not threaten; but he trusted to him who judges justly. He himself bore our sins in his body on the tree, that we might die to sin and live to righteousness. By his wounds you have been healed. For you were straying like sheep, but have now returned to the Shepherd and Guardian of your souls.

Likewise you wives, be submissive to your husbands, so that some, though they do not obey the word, may be won without a word by the behavior of their wives, when they see your reverent and chaste behavior. Let not yours be the outward adorning with braiding of hair, decoration of gold, and wearing of fine clothing, but let it be the hidden person of the heart with the imperishable jewel of a gentle and quiet spirit, which in God's sight is very pre-

ce the holy women who hoped in God used to adorn
and were submissive to their husbands, as Sarah
raham, calling him lord. And you are now her children
right and let nothing terrify you.

Likewise you husbands, live considerately with your wives,
bestowing honor on the woman as the weaker sex, since you are
joint heirs of the grace of life, in order that your prayers may not
be hindered.

(I Pet. 2:18—3:7)

In comparison to Paul, Peter is far more patriarchal and tied to his
Hebrew tradition. His version of the household code that Paul used
twice in his letters lays heavier stress on the subordinate and deferen-
tial role of women, as well as that of slaves. He had nothing to say to
slave masters.

The principle Peter enunciated was "Be subject for the Lord's sake
to every human institution." This is rather different from Paul's principle of mutual deference irrespective of social status.

Peter's letters are far less localized than Paul's, being addressed to
Christians of Jewish origin among the dispersion "in Pontus, Galatia,
Cappadocia, Asia and Bithynia." His target audiences were in the east-
ern half of the Roman empire. Like Paul, Peter was particularly concerned with those wives who became Christians while their husbands
did not. No doubt he shared Paul's concern that Christianity not be
charged with an anti-family bias, nor any anti-government activism.

His Old Testament model of Sarah would hardly appeal to twentieth-century Christians. After all, did she not encourage Abraham to
take her slave girl, Hagar, and have a son by her, rather than believe
God would work a miracle and cause her to have a son in her old age?
In many other ways, Sarah was less than an ideal wife.

The problem with Peter was that he had nothing at all to say to the
husband, whereas, as we saw, Paul insisted the husband imitate Christ's
self-sacrifice in the way he loved his wife. Peter loaded slaves with
that responsibility!

Writer to the Hebrews

By faith Sarah herself received power to conceive, even when she
was past the age, since she considered him faithful who had prom-

ised. Therefore from one man, and him as good as dea
descendants as many as the stars of heaven and as
able grains of sand by the seashore.

The unknown author of this letter set forth examples from the Old
Testament of faithful obedience to God. Sarah came in for mention because she believed God would do the impossible and cause her to give
birth well after her normal cycle of fertility had passed. This was a
strange example, given the Genesis (chapter 18) account of Sarah
laughing at the idea that she and her husband were capable of being
sexually active at their age, and then encouraging Abraham to take her
slave girl to bed to have the promised son. However, our unknown
author obviously believed that agreeing to try to conceive at such an
advanced age was evidence of Sarah's commitment to God's will.

> By faith the walls of Jericho fell down after they had been encir-
> cled for seven days. By faith Rahab the harlot did not perish with
> those who were disobedient, because she had given friendly wel-
> come to the spies.
>
> *(Heb. 11:30-31)*

Rahab certainly stands out as a woman who, in spite of her trade, was
prepared to trust in the God of the Jews. She later married Salmon and
gave birth to the Boaz who married Ruth, and is mentioned in Matthew's genealogy of Jesus. James also refers to Rahab in his letter,
using her as an example where good works prove the existence of faith
in God (Jas. 2:25).

Neither the writer to the Hebrews nor James says anything about
the place of women in the church.

It can be seen, then, that the main defendant of the right of women to
take a full and equal part with men in the life and work of the early
church was Paul of Tarsus. He is often maligned as being a misogynist.
But I hope I have shown that, for his day, Paul was far ahead of his
culture and his own Jewish upbringing.

However, as I will show, even what Paul achieved was soon to be
ripped apart, to the extent that women disappear almost entirely from
the leadership and work of the church.

seven

Women in the Post-Apostolic Era

I want now to mention just a few of the later developments to show how women rapidly became excluded from leadership in the church, except for the formation of the orders of deaconess and widow—a device for keeping women firmly under the control of the male hierarchy.

The Apostolic Fathers

This collection of documents dates from the early second century and consists mostly of letters written by bishops to congregations around the empire. There are thirteen of these letters, mostly rather long ones. There are three other lengthy documents that are either sermons or teachings.

In only one of these—the letter of Ignatius to Smyrna—is there any mention by name of women; they are Gavia and Alce, both personal friends of the author. The only time women are mentioned is to tell them to be submissive to their husbands!

First Epistle of Clement of Rome to the Corinthians

He reminds the Corinthian Christians that:

> . . . your womenfolk were bidden to go about their duties in irre-
> proachable devotion and purity of conscience, showing all proper
> affection to their husbands; they were taught to make obedience
> the rule of their lives, to manage their households decorously, and
> to be patterns of discretion in every way.
>
> *(1:3)*

Not content with a reminder of what they had already been taught, he goes on to exhort them to:

> ... set our womenfolk on the road to goodness, by teaching them to be examples of lovable purity, to display real sincerity in their submissiveness, to prove the self-restraint of their tongues by observing silence, and to bestow equal affection, with no favoritism and as becomes holiness, upon all God-fearing persons.
>
> *(XXI:6-7)*

Bishop Clement of Rome is certainly not in the mode of the apostle Paul whom he was pleased to quote when it suited him. Women, for him, and especially Corinthian women, were to be kept in the background, where they were before early Christianity had begun to liberate them.

The Epistle of Ignatius to the Smyrnaeans

At the very end he sends greetings "to the families of my brethren who have wives and children; and to those virgins whom you call widows." It seems strange to single out those men who are married. Did this mean Ignatius believed Christian men should remain single, or that he devalued marriage?

The virgins here were probably single unattached women who had no male sponsors, had remained unmarried and were included among those who were in need of special care and attention, not being able to earn their own living.

He sends special greetings to "Gavia and her family," with prayers that she continue being faithful and steadfast in her church and community work. He also greets Alce, "who is specially dear to me." He referred to her later in his letter to Polycarp. These are the only mentions of women by name in the Apostolic Fathers.

The Epistle of Ignatius to Polycarp

Polycarp was a bishop at Smyrna and was to become one of the best known of the early Christian martyrs.

Polycarp issues some instructions, including:

> Let not widows be neglected. After the Lord be thou their protector.

Then the following:

> Tell my sisters to love the Lord, and to content themselves
> physically and spiritually with their own husbands.
>
> *(V)*

This kind of instruction is not given to husbands. But he does go on
to say:

> In like manner also charge my brothers in the name of Jesus
> Christ to love their wives, as the Lord loves the church.

He sends greetings to the unnamed wife of a local civic official, and
again to Alce.

The Epistle of Polycarp to the Philippians

Polycarp, Bishop of Smyrna, on his way to Rome where he was eventually to be martyred, had been asked by the church at Philippi whether
anyone could deliver their letter to the Christians at Antioch in Syria.
They also asked for copies of Ignatius' letters. Polycarp sends this letter as a covering note with copies of Ignatius' letters.

He was very much in the mold of Ignatius when it came to women.

> After that we can go on to instruct our womenfolk in the tradi-
> tions of the faith, and in love and purity; teaching them to show
> fondness and fidelity to their husbands, and a chaste and impar-
> tial affection for everyone else, and to bring up their children in
> the fear of God. Widows are to observe discretion as they prac-
> tice our Lord's faith; they should make constant intercessions for
> everyone, and be careful to avoid any tale-bearing, spiteful tittle-
> tattle, false allegations, over-eagerness for money, or misconduct
> of any description. They are to recognize that they are an altar of
> God, who scrutinizes every offering laid on it, and from whom
> none of their thoughts or intentions—no single one of their heart's
> secrets—can be hidden.
>
> *(IV:2-3)*

> The conduct of our young women, equally (with the young men),
> must show the unblemished purity of their conscience.
>
> *(V:3)*

Here again was the stereotyping of females Jesus and Paul had
avoided. Where once women were allowed to be themselves in their

own right, they were now back in their subservient role. They were once more the source of sexual sin and were to keep themselves and their conscience absolutely pure. I find it interesting that only women were exhorted to have this inner spiritual and moral purity. This is typical of the Mediterranean model I outlined at the beginning of this book, where the women's role was to have that sense of shame used to protect men from losing their honor. Pure women, you see, made sure men did not sin; impure women resulted in men who did sin. Men are thus the victims of women's sexuality.

It can be seen that, in the Apostolic Fathers as a whole, women were very much an inferior caste and a potential source of promiscuity and factionalism in the church. Only two are mentioned by name and one is unnamed, the wife of an official.

The contrast with the apostolic era is obvious and tragic.

It was almost inevitable that, once ordained clergy came into being and authority was centered around a monarchical bishop, lay involvement in the mission and leadership of the church would disappear. But not only did the work of women disappear—other than in service to the community through prayer and the care of widows—their actual status as wives and single women reverted to what it was in pre-Christian times.

The Didache

This document was known only by reference to it in several early Christian works. It did not come to light until the late nineteenth century when it was accidentally discovered in the library of the patriarch at Constantinople.

It is known simply as "Didache" which is Greek for "teaching," and claims to be an official collection of basic Christian teachings handed on by the twelve apostles.

The first half is a sermon-like feature called "The Two Ways," that is, the way of life and the way of death. It reads like exhortations of a father to his son. The only references to women here are as follows:

≤ abortion is forbidden
≤ discipline both sons and daughters in the fear of the Lord
≤ don't shout at male or female domestic slaves.

The second section is a kind of church manual, containing rules for the organization and worship within the congregation. The whole tenor of this manual is thoroughly masculine. There is absolutely no account taken of the possibility that a prophet or teacher or deacon could be a woman. Women do not rate a single mention.

Thus women as leaders and workers disappear almost entirely from the church. The only time they emerge is in a group of documents that are more like romantic novels. It seems that these documents, known as "Apocryphal Acts," could have been written from within communities of sexually inactive women as a protest against the disappearance of female leadership and ministry from the church as a whole.

What did remain were two subordinate orders—deaconesses and widows—that were set up to keep these women under male control. Their only avenue of service was to help the all-male ministry, and to do some social service.

The other documents that have come down to us from gnostic sources invariably describe women as becoming male.

Eusebius' History of the Church

Writing in the early fourth century of our era, Bishop Eusebius of Caesarea wrote out as best he could with the resources available to him a history of the church from the birth of Christ to the reign of Constantine. Many of the documents he referred to have not survived, and so the accuracy of his quotations cannot always be checked.

Reading through the early sections where he detailed the history of the church from the death of the last apostle, you soon discover that no women are mentioned in connection with the work and leadership of the church.

When Eusebius wrote, instead of being a motley collection of house churches with no central leadership structures, the church had become centralized around the bishop of a large city, with the bishop of Rome starting to claim primacy. One of the results of this is that lay leadership and participation in congregational life had virtually disappeared, with women receiving no mention at all.

There is a lengthy quote from a document sent from Gaul, describing the martyrdoms of four people: Sanctus, Maturus, Attalus and

Blandina. The last one was a woman and the account credits her with being the most noble of them all, encouraging the others to remain firm. But Blandina is the only woman mentioned in this post-apostolic period. Eusebius is interested mainly in the bishops, for the history of the bishops is the history of the church. In many respects he did his history the same way his Greek and Roman predecessors had: by concentrating on the leaders as though the people had no history of their own.

Even when dealing with the apostolic period, few, if any, women are mentioned by name, other than Mary, mother of Christ. The difference between Eusebius' account and the New Testament documents is immense when it comes to the naming of women.

What began as a movement that offered dignity and equality to women ended up as an organization that was almost totally androcentric.

The Apocryphal Writings

At the same time women disappeared from church life, there emerged a spate of Christian writings that were full of women and their daring deeds. The second and third centuries seemed to spawn these fictional accounts of the life of Christ and the apostles, as well as some religious novels.

One scholar has suggested that the writers of these documents were in fact widows. Why widows? Well, married women would not have had the time to do much writing, and I have no doubt their husbands would not have allowed them to write in such a triumphant way about women.

I will now give you a summary of the accounts of some of these women and their outrageous actions. I myself have no doubt these stories were a kind of backlash against the deliberate exclusion of women from the leadership of the church. As the canonical writings of the New Testament became more widely circulated, women would have been amazed at how important a role they played in the earlier generations of their church. Being powerless to correct this, they could easily have found an outlet in writing in the name of some well-known male leader or apostle. They certainly could not write in their own name, for to do so would have been to make sure their work was burned!

The Protevangelion of James

The Virgin Mary must have parents, so two are invented for her: Joachim and Anna. They are under a cloud of shame because Anna is childless. Two angels appear to Anna and promise her a child, who is to be called Mary. The child is offered to the priests at the temple while Anna sings a song reminiscent of the "Magnificat of Mary."

When Mary is three years old she is taken to the temple and is educated there while being fed by an angel. At twelve she is miraculously betrothed to Joseph, starts weaving a purple veil for the temple and has an angelic visitation promising her motherhood of the Messiah.

After the birth of Jesus, a woman named Salome, whose hand had withered because she did not believe the midwife's story of the Virgin Mary giving birth, has her hand restored when she goes into the cave where Mary and Jesus are and reaches out to touch the child.

Thus, the whole focus of this story is on Mary and not on either Joseph or Jesus.

Infancy Gospels

A variety of writings claiming to come from either Mary or an apostle began to circulate in the late second century. The following is a summary of the main stories concerning women, mostly to do with Mary.

An old Hebrew woman takes Jesus' foreskin after his circumcision and preserves it in an alabaster box of oil and spikenard—the very box that was used later by the prostitute when she anointed Jesus.

Mary hangs out one of Jesus' swaddling clothes after washing it; a young boy touches it and has his demons exorcised. Mary exorcises a young woman by merely showing her pity. She hands the baby Jesus to a young bride who had been struck dumb by a demon and heals her. She does the same thing for another young woman who is invaded by Satan. This woman then brings some scented water and washes Jesus with it, then sprinkles some on a young woman who has leprosy and heals her. A princess who has given birth to a leprous child, on hearing this story, does the same and her son is healed. She brings gifts to Mary in thanks. Many other similar miracles are performed by Mary, using water with which she had bathed Jesus.

The rest of the account is replete with miracles performed by Mary.

The Acts of Paul and Thecla

An early church father claimed *The Acts of Paul and Thecla* was written by an orthodox presbyter of Asia. But the inclusion of a woman, Thecla, who had such a prominent role in this narrative, would be most unlikely, especially from such a legitimate source. Paul is a minor character in this narrative.

Here is a summary of her part: Onesiphorus of Iconium invites Paul to preach to the congregation meeting in his house. A virgin named Thecla, whose mother is Theoclea and who is betrothed to Thamyris, is eventually converted by Paul. When Paul is imprisononed as the result of a plot, Thecla bribes her way into the prison and kisses his chains.

Later, Thecla is brought before the governor to explain why she now refuses to marry Thamyris. She says nothing and is condemned to be burned at the stake. She has a vision of Christ and the fires do not touch her because God causes an earthquake and a downpour of rain. She joins Paul as his virgin companion.

Because she refused the advances of Alexander, a magistrate, she is condemned to be thrown to wild beasts. Meanwhile, she is adopted by Trifina, whose daughter has just died. This is to ensure her virginity until she meets the wild beasts. Trifina accompanies Thecla to the amphitheater where the wild beasts are given a chance to lick her feet.

When Thecla is finally stripped naked and thrown among the beasts, they all bow down to her. She jumps into the pool of carnivorous fish but they all die. The authorities try every trick to incite a range of wild beasts to attack Thecla, but nothing works. Finally, Trifina dies and the governor calls for Thecla to find out who she really is. Thecla then proclaims her faith in Christ and she is released. Trifina miraculously returns to life and takes Thecla to her home, where many young women are converted to Christ.

Thecla finds Paul and tells him all that has happened to her. She then returns to Iconium to find Thamyris is now dead but her own mother still living. She is unable to persuade her to become a Christian, so she goes off to a mountain retreat and founds a monastic order.

Priests of the cult of Diana hatch a plot to kill her, but she is saved by a miraculous earthquake. She is translated to heaven at the age of ninety.

There are hardly any points at which this novel touches on anything that happened to the Paul of the New Testament. It seems unlikely that an orthodox presbyter of the second century could have written this for an ordinary congregation. Thecla, and not Paul, is the hero. She acts extraordinarily outrageous and is divinely protected in ways not given to men.

Written at a time when women had altogether disappeared from the leadership of the church, it is more likely to have been an attack on the male dominance of the church ministry.

The Acts of John

The central part of this story is given over to the adventures of one Drusiana, wife of Andronicus. She suffers many things, even death, in her bid to remain true to her faith and her husband. She is resurrected, along with some others, by John.

The point here is that this woman is being set forth as a true exemplar of the Christian faith. No men are so written about in this novel other than John himself.

The Acts of Peter

Simon the magician enters secretly the house of Eubula, a rich woman, and steals her jewels. Peter is told about this and there begins a long and involved story about how the jewels are recovered. Eubula responds by selling all her jewelry and giving the proceeds for the poor, the widows and the orphans, and by committing her heart to the Lord Jesus. She eventually dies in peace.

The mother of a senator pleads for her dead son to be restored to life. Peter raises him up and she gives him 4,000 pieces of gold for the care of widows.

Another rich woman, Chryse, gives Peter 10,000 pieces of gold.

In Rome, Xanthippe, wife of Caesar's friend Albinus, leads a delegation of wives to see Peter, telling him they have left their husband's beds in order to worship God in sobriety and cleanness.

Once again, women are portrayed as exemplars, not men.

The Acts of Thomas

The ninth act in this story concentrates on Mygdonia, wife of Charisius, right hand man of the king Gundaphorus of India.

She hears Thomas and becomes a disciple. This results in her deciding to have no further sexual relations with her husband. He tries everything he knows to persuade her back into his bed, but does not succeed.

Charisius then persuades the king to imprison Thomas after scourging him with 128 blows. But even this does not get him his wife back. She steals some money to try bribing the prison guards to let Thomas out, but Thomas has already been let out miraculously and meets her. She finally receives baptism.

Still more humiliations await her, but in the process two other women, Tertai and Narcia are converted.

Thomas is back in prison and now the three women are imprisoned. Thomas is finally martyred. The husbands of Mygdonia and Narcia fail to get them back into their beds and finally leave them in peace to live their lives in chastity.

Apart from Thomas, women are the heroes and exemplars of Christian living in this story.

The Acts of Xanthippe and Polyxena

This fourth-century narrative is centered around two prominent women of Spain.

Xanthippe is the wife of Probus, a man of rank, and Polyxena is her sister. She hears about Paul from one of her slaves who had just returned from Rome where Paul was staying. This starts her on a season of prayer to God for enlightenment and for an opportunity to meet this Paul.

Her prayers are answered when Paul arrives in Spain and goes to her city. Probus goes out, finds Paul and brings him to the house. On seeing him, Xanthippe falls down before him and wipes his feet with her hair.

When she asks for baptism from Paul, however, her husband shuts him out of the house and keeps her in her bedroom. But she escapes by bribing a slave, finds Paul in the house of Philotheus and is baptized. She then has a vision of Christ appearing to her. Soon her husband comes in search of her and is also baptized.

Polyxena then wishes to find faith. She has several terrible adventures with demons and wild animals and is finally baptized by Paul, as was her suitor and another man who had sought to carry her off.

This is another story typical of that period. Its focus is again on women as heroes and exemplars of the true faith.

There are many other instances of women heroes in this apocryphal literature. There can be no doubt they were written into the narratives to encourage women to be brave and rise above the invisibility that had been laid over them by the male hierarchy of the church. The writers were careful to portray the apostles as encouraging these women heroes to return to their husbands, so as not to be seen to be devaluing marriage.

But there was an awful dilemma being placed on married women during this period. On the one hand the ideal Christian life was portrayed as one that included sexual continence. On the other hand, women married to non-Christian husbands found it impossible to fulfill this ideal without divorce—a solution not favored by the church.

So we find these stories centering around married women who suffer greatly for the right to remain continent yet stay married to their non-Christian husbands.

Thus, rebellion is being encouraged in women through this fictional literature.

The Apostolic Constitutions

Jump ahead a century or so and the reality of the place of women in the church comes to light. This document is written in the name of "the apostles and elders" and is addressed to "all those who from among the gentiles have believed in the Lord Jesus Christ."

The text is actually from the late fourth century of our era, with many of its "canons" accepted by one or two universal church councils.

The role of women is dealt with in several places throughout this long document, so I will take them in the order in which they occur.

There is a long diatribe against the "strange and wicked woman" who will lure innocent young men into her bed, taken mainly from the Book of Proverbs. Needless to say, there are no warnings to women about wicked men!

Next, "let the wife be obedient to her husband," taken out of I Corinthians. This is followed by the account of the virtuous women in

Proverbs 31. The good wife is not to overadorn herself and force other men to take notice of her. You see how men have always been suckers for beautiful women: doesn't it remind you of the argument against women priests and how the poor men in the congregation will have their minds on her body instead of on the Lord?

Women must not attend the public baths when men are bathing there. They must avoid bathing in the middle of the day; rather they must go at the tenth hour of the day, and certainly not every day.

Women must not be contentious. "It is better to dwell in the wilderness, than with a contentious and angry woman." (Proverbs 21:19) Men, of course, are never contentious!

Widows come under even greater scrutiny than was given them in I Timothy. It is clear that an order of widows has been established. Widows under sixty years of age ought not be admitted, since they may remarry because of their sexual appetite and thus bring dishonor to the order. These younger women should be assisted and supported so that they may not remarry. Second marriages are a breach of the original marriage vows and third marriages are a sign of incontinence, while subsequent marriages are clear signs of fornication and licentiousness. The very young widows should be allowed one marriage to help them escape foolish lusts. There seems to be nothing said about men remarrying as many times as they wish.

Women are not allowed to teach in the church, only to pray and listen to men teaching. Widows are to stay in their own houses and not visit the houses of other people, especially those of unbelievers.

There follows a long diatribe against widows who behave in unseemly ways. Again, I am struck by the fact that no such diatribe is aimed at widowers.

Widows are to accept alms only from the faithful, and be ready to obey the clergy.

Women must not be ordained to the priesthood, as in the pagan religions, and they must not baptize. This is in the context of forbidding the laity generally to do anything the clergy are ordained to do.

Widows are to pray for those who help them, and women — especially deaconesses — are not to publish abroad their own good deeds.

When a woman is baptized, a deaconess must assist to reduce the physical contact between baptizer and baptized.

Virgins who take a vow of perpetual virginity must behave suitably. Again, no such commands are laid upon men who might take such a vow.

Again, wives are to be subject to their husbands, and husbands are to love their wives as partners in life and fellow helpers in the procreation of children.

In the directions about ordination services, the prayer for the ordination of a deaconess contains the words "cleanse her from all filthiness of flesh and spirit." These or similar words are not used in any services for ordaining men.

"He who has taken a widow, or a divorced woman, or a harlot, or a slave, or one belonging to the theater, cannot be either a bishop, priest or deacon, or indeed any one of the sacerdotal catalogue. He who has married two sisters, or his brother's or sister's daughter, cannot be a clergyman."

It can be clearly seen from this document that the position of women in the church had greatly deteriorated since apostolic times. The sadness is that a great deal of the attitudes behind such regulations still persist in many sections of the church today.

Conclusion

The evidence from all sources is unequivocal: while women of any social status were welcomed and encouraged to take an active part in the
life and leadership of the church during the first two generations of
Christianity, they virtually disappear for the next several generations.

The pattern is so clear as to require no great research. Jesus af-
firmed women as individuals in their own right without the social necessity of being under the control of a male sponsor. He was honored
to have rich women organize the food and accommodation of his male
disciples and himself when they journeyed around Galilee. God even
chose women to be the first to know of the coming of the Messiah, and
to be the first to see and hear the Risen Christ.

Paul was happy to have women work side-by-side with him in his
missionary work around Greece. He was comfortable with women being the head of housegroups of worshiping Christians. He did have
some problems with a few women in places where the outside world
considered women inferiors and sex objects, but overall he clearly encouraged women to take a full part in the spiritual work of the church.
The only deacon named is a woman, Phoebe.

And then, at the end of the first century of our era, women dropped
out of sight in the leadership and work of the church. The only exceptions were a few very powerful Christian women from the ruling
classes. Some of these were widowed early in life and were able to use
the resources inherited from their husbands to care for widows and
orphans.

It seems there was an excess of elite Christian women with no men of similar status to marry. This allowed them to maintain their social status and exert some influence on the church.

But they were not allowed to participate in the ordained ministry, and therefore had no say in policy making. It needs to be remembered that by the turn of the first century, lay participation in church leadership had almost disappeared, so there was never any hope for women.

There has been some speculation that an order of deaconesses emerged, derived from Phoebe the deacon of Cenchreae. It has even been suggested that the widows of I Timothy 5:9 may have been deaconesses. However, in dealing with the passage earlier, I pointed out how the word that is translated as "enrolled" really means "considered" and that Paul was defining those who could be categorized as true widows rather than having them enrolled in a list.

Orders of deaconesses and widows did emerge a century or two later, probably in response to the growing numbers of unattached women and the problem of how to manage their care. But these "orders" were firmly under the control of the bishops and were allowed to do only those things men generally preferred not to do.

The immediate post-apostolic era shows clear evidence of women being put back into their pre-Christian roles.

And then in the wealth of apocryphal literature that emerged from the second to the fourth centuries, women were portrayed as heroes and exemplars. There is good reason to believe such literature was brought into being by rich and powerful women who may have endowed male writers to create these stories as a protest against the disappearance of women from the history of the church.

From then until the protestant reformations and the catholic counter reformation, women continued in their inferior and submissive roles.

Just as the growth of the lay ministry among mainstream churches is only a hundred or so years old, so the movement for recognizing the ministry of women is relatively recent outside of religious orders. Even in those denominations that have allowed ordained women to take part in the life and leadership of the church, they are still placed in roles subservient to the male clergy.

I believe the Holy Spirit is awakening and empowering women in all the churches to arise and re-establish their place in the church.

If this means being somewhat outrageous, recall all the outrageous women in the gospels and the early church who defied convention, knowing God was even more outrageous than they in concentrating on the poor and the powerless, offering them full and equal membership in the kingdom of God, even if that meant defying a whole range of human social conventions.

Indeed, these are exciting times.

Appendix

References in the New Testament (NT), Apostolic Fathers, New Testament Apocrypha

Adulteress
NT
Jn. 8:3-11

Anna
NT
Lk. 2:36-38

Apphia
NT
Philem. 2

Bernice
NT
Acts 25:13

Chloe
NT
I Cor. 1:11

Claudia
NT
II Tim. 4:21

Crippled Woman
NT
Lk. 13:10-17

Damaris
NT
Acts 17:34

Drusilla
NT
Acts 24:24

Elizabeth
NT
Lk. 1:5, 7, 13, 24, 36, 40, 41, 57
NT APOCRYPHA
Gospel of the Ebionites, 3
Protevangelium of James, 12.2-3; 21.3
Pistis Sophia, c.7
Life of John According to Serapion, p. 414-5 (Hennecke, Schneemelcher *et al.*)

Euodia and Syntyche
NT
  Phil. 4:2

Herodias and Salome
NT
  Mat. 14:3, 6
  Mk. 6:17, 19, 22
  Lk. 8:19

Indigent Widow
NT
  Mk. 12:41-44
  Lk. 21:1-4

Julia
NT
  Rom. 16:15

Junia
NT
  Rom. 16:7

Lois and Eunice
NT
  II Tim. 1:5

Lydia
NT
  Acts 16:14-15, 40

Maid Who Challenged Peter
NT
  Mat. 26:69-75
  Lk. 22:54-60
  Jn. 18:16-18

Mary and Martha
NT
  Lk. 10:38-42
  Jn. 11:1-45; 12:1-8
NT APOCRYPHA
  Epistle of the Apostles, 8-9

Mary of Magdala
NT
  Mat. 27:56, 61; 28:1
  Mk. 15:40, 47; 16:1, 9
  Lk. 8:2; 24:10
  Jn. 19:25; 20:1,11-18
APOSTOLIC FATHERS
Fragments of Papias, 1
NT APOCRYPHA
  Gospel of Peter, 12.50-57
  Epistle of the Apostles,
    10-11
  Gospel of Thomas, Logion 114
  Gospel According to Mary,
    PBerol. p.9.12-20; p.17.17-22;
    p.18.1-21

Mary Mother of Jesus
NT
  Mat. 1:16, 18-19, 20; 2:11, 13-23;
    12:46-50; 13:55
  Mk. 3:31, 6:3
  Lk. 1:26-56; 2:5, 16, 19, 34, 41-
    51; 8:19-21
  Jn. 2:1-5, 12; 6:42; 19:25-27
Acts 1:14
APOSTOLIC FATHERS
Fragments of Papias, 10
NT APOCRYPHA
  Gospel of the Hebrews, 1
  Epistle of the Apostles, 3-5; 14-15
  Protevangelium of James, 5.2-
    21.3
  Infancy Story of Thomas, p.400-
    401 (Hennecke, Schneemelcher
    et al.)
  Arabic Infancy Gospel,
    23-4, 40
  Gospel of Pseudo-Matthew, 23,
    73

Witnesses of Jesus'
Resurrection
NT
  Mat. 28:1-10
  Mk. 16:1-8, 9-11
  Lk. 23:55-6; 24:1-11
  Jn. 20:1-18

Woman Who Celebrated
Womanhood
NT
  Lk. 11:27-28

Woman Who Lost a Coin
NT
  Lk. 15:8-10

Woman With an Issue of
Blood
NT
  Mat. 9:20-2
  Mk. 5:25-34
  Lk. 8:43-48

Women Patrons
NT
  Mat. 27:55-56
  Mk.15:40-41
  Lk. 8:1-3

Women Who Anointed Jesus
NT
  Mat. 26:6-13
  Mk. 14:3-9
  Lk. 7:36-50
  Jn. 12:1-8

Women Who Mourned on the
Way to the Cross
NT
  Lk. 23:26-32

Further Reading

The Social Background

Esler, P. F., *The First Christians in the Social Worlds: Social-Scientific Approaches to New Testament Interpretation*, Routledge, 1994

Judge, E. A., *The Social Pattern of Christian Groups in the First Century*, Tyndale Press, 1960

Leming, M. R., DeVries, R. G., and Furnish, B. F. J. eds., *The Sociological Perspective: A Value-committed Introduction*, Zondervan, 1989

Malina, B. J., *The New Testament World: Insights from Cultural Anthropology*, SCM, 1981

Pilch, J. J. and Malina, B. J. eds., *Biblical Social Values and Their Meaning: A Handbook*, Hendrickson, 1993

Theissen, G., *The First Followers of Jesus: A Sociological Analysis of the Earliest Christianity*, SCM, 1978

—*The Social Setting of Pauline Christianity*, T & T Clark, 1982

The Place of Women

Davies, S. L., *The Revolt of the Widows: the Social World of the Apocryphal Acts*, SIUP, 1980

Dixon, S., *The Roman Mother*, Routledge, 1990

Fiorenza, E. S., *In Memory of Her: A Feminist Theological Reconstruction of Christian Origins*, SCM, 1983

Fox, R. L., *Pagans and Christians*, Penguin, 1986

Heine, S., *Women and Early Christianity: Are the Feminists Scholars Right?*, SCM, 1987

Jensen, A., *God's Self-Confident Daughters Westminster*, John Knox Press, 1996

Laffey, A. L., *Wives, Harlots and Concubines: The Old Testament in Feminist Perspective*, Fortress Press, 1988

Lefkowitz, M. R. and Fant, M. B. eds., *Women's Life in Greece and Rome: A Sourcebook in Translation*, Duckworth, 1982

Pomeroy, S. B., *Goddesses, Whores, Wives, and Slaves: Women in Classical Antiquity*, Pimlico, 1975

Ryrie, C. C., *The Role of Women in the Church*, Moody Press, 1958

Stagg, E. and F., *Woman in the World of Jesus*, Saint Andrew Press, 1978

Witherington III, B. *Women in the Ministry of Jesus*, CUP, 1984

— *Women and the Genesis of Christianity*, CUP, 1990

General Reference

Eusebius, *The History of the Church*. Trans. Williamson, G. A., Penguin, 1965

Freyne, S., *The World of the New Testament*, Veritas Publications, 1980

Hennecke, E., Schneemelcher, W. and Wilson, R. eds., *New Testament Apocrypha*, Westminster Press, 1963

James, M. R., *The Apocryphal New Testament*, Clarendon, 1924

The Apostolic Constitutions in *The Ante-Nicene Fathers*, Vol.VII, T & T Clark, 1994

Jeremias, J., *Jerusalem in the Time of Christ*, SCM, 1969

Malina, B. J. and Rohrbaugh, R L, *Social-Science Commentary on the Synoptic Gospels*, Fortress Press, 1992

Marshall, I. H., *Acts: An Introduction and Commentary*, Tyndale, 1980

Staniforth, M. and Louth, A. eds., *Early Christian Writings: The Apostolic Fathers*, Penguin, 1969

Endnotes

1. Matthew 13:53-58; Mk. 6:1-6; Lk. 4:16-30
2. Protevangelion of James 1.2-4 *New Testament Apocrypha* ed. Hennecke and Schneemelcher.
3. Mark 10:2-12
4. *Antiquities of the Jews* 18.5
5. Luke 15:4-7
6. Acts 1:14
7. John 19:26-7
8. Acts 2:14
9. Acts 5:14
10. Acts 8:3
11. Acts 6:5
12. Acts 8:4-13
13. Acts 8:26-39
14. Acts 8:40
15. p.4
16. 1 Corinthians 11:5
17. *New Documents Illustrating Early Christianity* Vol. 4 p.239

Index

Other Seastone Titles

Music of Silence
David Steindl-Rast with Sharon Lebell
Introduction by Kathleen Norris

A noted Benedictine monk shows us how to incorporate the sacred meaning of monastic life into our everyday world by paying attention to the "seasons of the day" and the enlivening messages to be found in each moment. *Trade paper. $12.00*

4000 Years of Christmas: A Gift from the Ages
Earl W. Count and Alice Lawson Count
Introduction by Dan Wakefield

Tracing myths and folklore from the Near East to northern Europe, *4000 Years of Christmas* reveals the surprising origins of our modern Christmas holiday. With flowing narrative and decorative illustrations, this book embarks on a journey across cultures and millennia to reveal a celebration that is at the heart of all humanity. *Hardcover. Two color throughout. $16.00*

The Psalms in Haiku: Meditative Songs of Prayer
Father Richard Gwyn

Here are praises to spiritual power presented in a stark and clear fashion, in the ancient Japanese form of haiku poetry. These vivid and deeply moving versions will challenge those familiar with the Psalms to look for new meaning while introducing the prayers to a whole new audience. *Trade paper. $14.00*

The Life of Mary and Birth of Jesus: The Ancient Infancy Gospel of James
Ronald F. Hock

Of Mary's biography, the New Testament tells us little. Yet scenes from her life decorate churches around the world and are well known to her admirers. The source of these stories is a little-known manuscript that tells the entire story of Mary's life. Here is the complete text together with reproductions of the artworks that illustrate the influence of this Gospel on Christian art. *Hardcover. $16.00.*

To order these or other Seastone books call 800-377-2542 or 510-601-8301, e-mail ulysses@ulyssespress.com or write to Ulysses Press, P.O. Box 3440, Berkeley, CA 94703-3440. There is no charge for shipping on retail orders. California residents must include sales tax. Allow two to three weeks for delivery.

About the Author

Ross Saunders is an Australian Anglican priest. He has twenty years of professional experience in broadcasting and is the author of numerous articles and documentaries.